Art Activities

Lynne Burgess

Published by Scholastic Publications Ltd,
Villiers House, Clarendon Avenue,
Leamington Spa, Warwickshire
CV32 5PR

© 1994 Scholastic Publications Ltd
Text © 1994 Lynne Burgess

Written by Lynne Burgess
Editor Noel Pritchard
Assistant Editor Kate Banham
Illustrator Rachel Conner
Photographs by Bob Bray (pages 5, 55 and
79), and Alex Leathley (page 17) (for the
Portsmouth City Arts Festival 1993)
Cover design by Lynne Joesbury
Cover photograph by Martyn Chillmaid
Children's artwork provided by
the children of Burwash County Primary
School and Maynards Green Primary
School, East Sussex

Every attempt has been made to trace and acknowledge the
origins of pre-published material and photographs appearing in
this book. The publishers apologise for any omissions.

Typeset by Typesetters (Birmingham) Ltd
Artwork by Steve Williams & Associates, Leicester
Printed at Alden Press Limited, Oxford and Northampton,
Great Britain

British Library Cataloguing in Publication Data
A catalogue record for this book is available from the British
Library

ISBN 0-590-53098-4

Contents

Introduction

Many early years teachers feel confident introducing young children to new media such as charcoal or oil pastels and helping them explore a new technique such as potato printing. Any difficulties can usually be solved by consulting one of the many books which cover these areas. However, while exploring new media and mastering techniques are an essential ingredient in the education of this age range, it is equally important to explore the 'art elements' (sometimes called 'visual or formal elements').

Art elements

This curious phrase was probably little known to early years teachers until the advent of the National Curriculum in which Key Stage 1 pupils are expected to 'explore the elements of art and design'. But what aspects of these 'elements' should we be introducing to young children?

'Art elements' is an umbrella term for referring to Line, Colour, Shape and Texture. Some books may also include Tone and Pattern as separate elements, but here they are referred to within the context of the other four main areas. For example, Tone can mean a range of variations of one colour or the way in which lines can be used to create light or dark areas. Similarly, Patterns can be made with lines, colours or shapes. Each art element can apply to work in both two and three dimensions.

Artists deliberately manipulate these elements in order to express their feelings and ideas. Children need to understand what these elements are and how they can use them in their own work in a more considered way. By the end of Key Stage 1, children should have 'explored' these elements but even pre-school and reception children can be introduced to them.

In some ways it is rather artificial to discuss the 'art elements' in isolation because they are inextricably linked to all the other strands in the National Curriculum. For example, if children are investigating light colours, they will inevitably be using some kind of media, such as paint, and some sort of technique, such as printing. They may also be drawing from observation, finding their own resources, modifying as they work and possibly relating their own work to other artists, designers and craftworkers. However, children are often repeatedly presented with the same media or technique without ever linking them to the art elements. For example, blowing paint with a straw is a common early years activity but frequently the emphasis is solely on the technique with no reference being made to how colours can mingle to create new ones. Hence, an important opportunity is missed, for young children need to experience these elements in a multitude of situations if they are to begin to understand them fully.

Similarly, it is unlikely that the art elements will be used completely separately in any art activity. For example, it is difficult to use colour without also using lines or shapes. However, because young children find it hard to concentrate on more than one or two variables at a time, it is worth focusing occasionally on one art element throughout the assignment. This is not to suggest that the whole of their art

point where structured activities are appropriate. Over a period of time, teachers need to ensure a balance between offering the child a totally free choice in subject matter, media and technique and more teacher-controlled learning situations.

The inspiration of other artists

Through exploring the 'art elements' in a less incidental way, young children will begin to develop a vocabulary which will enable them to talk more precisely not only about their own work but also in describing their responses to the work of others. This will help to build the bridge between the children's own work and that of adult artists, an essential strand in the Art National Curriculum.

Draw the children's attention to examples of art and design which can be found in their everyday environment. Look for the 'art elements' in local architecture, clothing, wallpaper, carpets, curtains, common household objects (such as mugs and furniture), book illustrations, posters and advertisements. Discuss how the artist has repeated a shape to form the pattern in a carpet or why the artist has chosen a particular colour theme for a poster. Whenever possible, look at the work of local living artists such as potters, weavers and architects. Ask them to show their work and talk to the children. Similarly, older pupils (junior, secondary or students in further education) could be asked to share their work with early years children. Broaden the children's experience of art by including examples from other cultures, past and present. Is it possible to compare the patterns on clothing (Indian saris) or shapes in floor tiles (Roman mosaics)?

experiences be structured solely around the 'art elements'. Exploring a new media or technique, or examining a particular subject matter, will often provide the starting-point to an activity. It is equally important to offer children activities which allow them the freedom to choose their own subject matter, media or technique without adult-imposed constraints. It is not necessary to provide isolated exercises to introduce this aspect of art. Many everyday activities in pre-school and reception classrooms offer ideal opportunities for highlighting the art elements.

When first introducing a new media or technique, young children do need a period to play and experiment to discover for themselves their potential without being limited to a specific task. It is vital pupils become confident in their use as well as understanding their characteristics. Most of the ideas in the main section of the book assume that children have already had ample opportunity to 'play' and have reached a

Link the children's exploration of the 'art elements' to examples of work by well known artists. Choose the example carefully to be sure that the use of line or texture will be easily descernible and will relate to the children's own experience. For example, if children have mixed their own colours and begun to develop a vocabulary to express what they see, they will find it much easier to discuss paintings by Monet or Turner. Young children have not acquired adult inhibitions about discussing a 'famous' work of art and are just as happy to talk about a picture by Van Gogh as a poster.

Teachers should not feel inhibited by their own lack of 'knowledge' because they will be using exactly the same questioning skills in discussing a famous painting as they would with a poster. Try a combination of 'closed' questions (What is the lady wearing?) and more 'open-ended' ones (What does it make you think of? How does it make you feel?).

As well as talking about the work of adult artists, young children can respond practically in a variety of ways:
● trying out the same techniques, such as using paint to mix similar colours;
● experimenting with the same media, such as black pens;
● exploring the same dominant 'art element', such as trying to create a similar texture or the same 'hot colours' used by the artist;
● responding in any media to the emotions conveyed in the picture by making their own version of someone crying or screaming;
● making their own version of the whole picture either using the same or different media. In this case, it is important to choose the picture carefully. Sometimes a picture with a strong, simple composition will be more successful because young children find it easier to distinguish the main component parts and include these in their own version.

The role of the teacher

Child art is a distinct phenomenon and should not be compared to adult art for each reflect a vastly different stage of thinking and understanding. It is easy to dismiss children's work as 'immature' and so not give it due credit. Early years teachers need to acknowledge this difference because it will help determine the kind of art experience offered to young children.

Individuality
No two children are alike and this should be reflected in their art work. There is no one 'right' answer but an infinite number of permutations, some perhaps more appropriate than others. Therefore, if the end product is predetermined — adult drawn outlines, templates, tracing, copying from magazines — then the activity cannot have any value for 'art education'.

If we acknowledge that child art is different from adult art, the imposition of adult images should be avoided. These can destroy children's confidence in their own abilities for it implies that they should try to achieve an image outside their perceptual development. It also assumes that children's thinking has to be done for them whereas true art activities should involve the child's intellectual powers as much as science or mathematics.

The teacher has a demanding task for, on the one hand, she must not be too heavily prescriptive, ignoring the individual's creative contribution, while on the other, it is unwise to allow totally free expression without any teaching of skills.

Process versus product
It is important to remember that the knowledge and understanding gained from the 'process' of an art activity is just as important as the 'end product'. Even if an end product has been unsuccessful for some reason, the child may well have gained information which will prove useful in some subsequent task. If we focus too heavily on the end product, it is easy to be over-prescriptive, producing images which merely please parents and other adults.

Working from direct experience
It is essential to use direct, firsthand experience as a stimulus for art activities as much as possible. Try to find objects which will excite children's innate curiosity and provide important sensory experiences. Close observation of a real object will generate far more effective art work than asking children to copy from books or rely on vague, distant memories — a task which most adults would find difficult.

Even very young children can be encouraged to look more carefully and include their observations in their pictures. For example, many may already have well-established 'schema' (personal symbols or individual marks/shapes used repeatedly) for drawing familiar things such as people, but these will be enriched and extended if children are encouraged to observe real people so they begin to notice details of the human figure such as ears, fingers, elbows and so on. They should not be expected to produce an exact replica but guided observation will often enable them to capture the 'essence' of a person or object.

Direct experience is not limited to work inspired by studying objects but can also include responses stimulated by people or events. When working from memory, it is wiser to use a fairly recent memory as a stimulus and, if possible, photographs and/or a discussion can revive the images locked in the mind.

Even work from imagination can be stimulated by direct observation. For example, if children are going to draw an imaginary teapot, show them a variety of teapots in different shapes, sizes and materials. Discuss each teapot in detail and ask questions to help them decide how their teapot will look. Helping children look carefully can feed their imagination and begin to develop a 'bank' of images on which to base future work.

Discussion

As with most early years activities, good quality work results more frequently when an adult supervises the activity and talks with the children. Many adults feel inhibited because of their own lack of skill in art but the function of the adult is not so much to demonstrate but to focus the children's attention, teach them to look in greater depth and help them express their observations orally. This is easily within the capabilities of all teachers for it is a skill which they readily use in teaching other subjects.

Spontaneity is a wonderful feature of young children's art work and is certainly something to be treasured. Teachers need to be sensitive to this when guiding children in their work. Discussion which

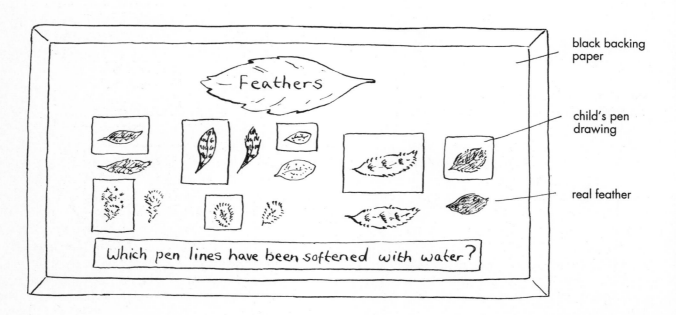

black backing paper

child's pen drawing

real feather

Feathers

Which pen lines have been softened with water?

encourages them to be more conscious of the choices open to them, extends and develops their abilities. However, we must be wary of accidentally imposing our own adult decisions and choices on them.

The majority of children are usually actively seeking adult approval and this applies particularly to their drawings. When a young child says 'I can't draw a picture of a fish', they sometimes mean 'I can't draw one which is as good as an adult's'. This lack of self-confidence can be overcome by showing that their own efforts are always valued. It can also mean 'I don't know where to start'. Through discussion based on a real fish, an adult can help structure the activity and break it down into more manageable steps. What is the main shape of the body? What other parts of the body are there and where do they join on to the main shape? How many eyes can you see? Are there any lines or marks on the fish? Questions such as these will help develop the strategy of starting with the large overall shapes first

and adding details later. It will also increase their self-confidence in tackling a task which they may initially feel is too daunting.

Display

It is important to celebrate young children's achievements by displaying their own efforts no matter how 'crude' they may appear to adults.

How their work is displayed will depend on the task set and the individual constraints presented by the classroom layout.

Often, two-dimensional work is most attractive if stapled directly on to a neutral coloured backing paper (black, grey or beige) so the eye is not distracted. Similarly, three-dimensional work is often best displayed at varying heights by placing different sized boxes under a neutral coloured fabric. Examples of both are shown below. Whenever possible, display the resources used to stimulate the activity or work which arose as part of the follow-up activities alongside the children's work.

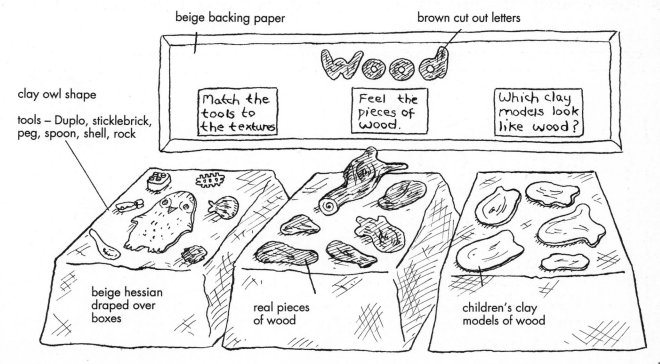

beige backing paper

brown cut out letters

clay owl shape

tools – Duplo, sticklebrick, peg, spoon, shell, rock

Match the tools to the textures

Feel the pieces of wood.

Which clay models look like wood?

beige hessian draped over boxes

real pieces of wood

children's clay models of wood

Progression

When planning art activities for early years pupils, the teacher needs to ensure continuity and progression. There are many facets to this task and it may be useful to consider the following points.

• Does the task match the children's level of concentration? Many pre-school pupils have very limited concentration spans and would need activities which could be completed relatively quickly or broken into several short sessions. However, Reception and Y1 children often have increased concentration spans and can work for a more sustained period.

• Will the activity allow the children to respond at their own developmental level? It is possible to identify distinct stages in the early development of children's image making (see Figure 1 and the introduction to the chapter on Line). Many pre-school and some reception children will still be at the random scribble stage where it is more beneficial to continue with activities which explore the media or technique. However, many Reception and Y1 children are developing recognisable images so more demanding tasks, such as working from observation, will encourage more sophisticated images.

• To what extent will the children be able to select resources, materials, media or equipment? When dealing with pre-school children (or those with little previous experience of art), the teacher is more likely to be making most of the decisions about the subject matter, which resources to offer, the type of fabric to be used, whether to glue or sew and which tools to provide. However, if children are to be capable of selecting their own resources and materials by the end of Key Stage 1, it is vital to involve them in helping to make these decisions as soon as possible. Initially, it may be wiser to offer them a limited choice (perhaps between two options) but as they increase in confidence, more choices can be provided. It is important to discuss why one choice is more appropriate than another.

• Will the media and techniques offered in the activity build on previous experiences and develop these further? Some media are much more difficult to handle successfully than others and it is important to bear this in mind. Offering chalks and charcoal may prove frustrating for children who have little experience of drawing with pencil or crayons. Similarly, some techniques demand much more physical co-ordination than others.

• Can the activity be designed to explore one of the 'art elements'? Once children are familiar with a particular media and technique, it is possible to focus on one particular aspect of an 'element'. Teachers may find it difficult to sequence such activities and so each chapter on Line, Shape, Colour and Texture discusses progression in the introduction and suggests activities which have been ordered according to difficulty. The activities have not necessarily been sequenced in order of difficulty for other aspects of art (media, technique, stage of development in image making and so on).

● How can the activity help children begin to review and modify their work? Children will need to develop 'art specific' vocabulary in order to discuss their own work (or others') so it is important to extend their language abilities by incorporating new words which relate to subject matter, media, technique and equipment. As well as developing their abilities to discuss, children need to be encouraged to begin to modify their work. Many pre-school children are satisfied with their first attempt at an activity and may be unlikely to want to alter it. However, as children mature (Reception and Y1), they begin to work in a more considered way and become more critical of their own work. These children can be encouraged to pay more attention to detail (drawing from observation), to handle media and techniques more proficiently (repeat a print to improve the quality) and to seek alternative solutions to problems (find another means of fixing a material to a model).

● Does the activity offer an opportunity to introduce children to the 'art' of others? Bear in mind that 'art' should be interpreted in its broadest sense to include everyday design (architecture, household objects, clothing), popular media (newspaper, magazines, advertisements, photographs, comics, book illustrations) as well as known artists (historical, contemporary and multicultural). Children should progress from gaining the confidence to talk about such 'art' to being able to relate specific aspects (subject matter, media, techniques) to their own work.

The introduction sections of each chapter outline the progression of skills which can be developed through the activities.

Resources

Gradually build up a collection of resources to support the study of other artists. Although it is far better for children to have direct firsthand experience of real art, secondary sources can also be of value.

Look out for everyday 'art' and collect examples of greetings cards, posters, advertisements, wallpaper, wrapping paper, curtain and carpet samples, fabrics, ceramics (jugs, teapots, mugs), cartoons and masks. Finding multicultural or historical examples may prove more difficult. Libraries may have a collection of books on art from different cultures or historical periods. Try local museums or galleries, some of which may provide a lending service to schools, and look in shops such as Oxfam (multicultural items) and Times Past (historical items).

Finding examples of well-known artists is slightly easier. Look not only in local libraries, museums and galleries but also at greetings cards, postcards and calendars. Shops such as Athena sell prints and some galleries (The Tate and The National Gallery, London) sell prints and posters by mail order.

Access to high-quality, three-dimensional work presents more problems. It is important for children to see real examples so they can touch them and experience them from all angles but in reality, this is not always possible. Rather than deny children any experience of three-dimensional art by famous artists, find examples in books, postcards, posters and photographs.

With any collection of resources, try to ensure a balance between male and female artists, two- and three-dimensional work, contemporary and historical and European and multicultural.

The structure of the book

No guide is given for the age suitability of any activity. The chronological age of a child is not as important as the developmental stage she has reached. For example, if a child is at the random scribble stage (see Figure 1), activities which involve exploring a particular medium are more appropriate. However, once a child can draw a simple circle with confidence, many of the activities which involve making images are now appropriate, especially if we accept that

their own attempts, no matter how primitive, are more valuable than drawing for them. For example, many children will be able to draw an umbrella (see page 73) even if the result is a simple rounded shape with a stick underneath. Although it may lack the sophistication of an adult image, it is much more meaningful to them than an adult drawing one for them.

Similarly, teachers will need to decide whether the activity will offer progression in terms of media and technique. Before choosing an activity, it is important to assess whether pupils have sufficient previous experience of the media or technique. If the media or technique are unfamiliar, it may be possible to simplify them slightly or design a series of activities to introduce them prior to the 'art element' activity.

The activities can often be adapted to link with a current project or area of study. For example, the activity based on Autumn leaves (see page 62) could be adapted to look at another colour family in a completely different subject such as the range of yellows in a group of toys or the variety of reds in a collection of clothing.

The activities include the following sections.

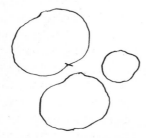

1. Random scribble.

2. Beginning circles.

3. Circles developing into schema for person.

4. Circles used in more mature schema for person.

Figure 1

14

Objective

This is the primary purpose of the activity but it may not necessarily be the only one. Many of the activities also make a contribution to other aspects of art education such as media, technique or critical studies. Within each chapter the suggested activities are sequenced in order of difficulty.

What you need

A list of the main materials and equipment needed is given for each activity. It is assumed that teachers will automatically protect working surfaces and provide aprons for the children when necessary. Similarly, it is important to ensure all materials are non-toxic and bear in mind children who may have allergies to any resources or materials. If a suggested task contains unfamiliar materials or techniques, it is important for the children to have an unstructured 'play' session with them before attemping the more structured activity. Remember to encourage them to help collect any resources to be used to inspire ideas (leaves, wrapping paper) or materials to be used in the activity (collections of boxes or fabrics).

Preparation

This section suggests activities which will introduce the children to the subject matter. Producing a box of unfamiliar objects and expecting young children to produce artwork based on them

immediately is an extremely demanding task. They need time to investigate and explore the objects. If possible, put them on display for several days and allow the children to handle them or study them through magnifying glasses. Hold brief discussion periods to encourage the children to describe their observations and help extend their vocabulary.

When choosing objects to help prepare for the activity, remember to include examples of everyday 'art' whenever relevant. If the children are looking for repeating patterns in clothing or wallpaper, have several examples available to show them. Whenever possible, include examples from other cultures or other periods of history.

Many of the suggested preparation activities can be carried out over several days with only a brief recap before beginning the assignment. A long preparation session immediately prior to an activity can cause very young children to feel tired or lose their enthusiasm. Teachers have a difficult balance to achieve for they need to provide enough stimulus before an activity while maintaining the children's interest in the task ahead.

What to do

Step-by-step instructions are given for each task but these can easily be adapted to suit your own circumstances and the needs of your particular pupils.

Initially, many children regard painting as a 'colouring in' exercise or use it to draw just as they would with a pencil. Once they have mastered the physical problems of manipulating the brush and the paint, they need to be encouraged to go back and paint on top of areas which they have already painted to add patterns, textures or fine details. Through this type of encouragement, they will begin to appreciate the full potential of paint as more than just another medium for drawing. Similarly, some of the activities suggest the children's work is cut out for the purposes of display. Some purists would suggest that cutting around children's work is best avoided because it can ruin all the energy which is a vital ingredient of work by this age range. However, if the children know that their artwork is to be cut out and mounted as part of a frieze and that they don't need to include a background, then it is a more acceptable practice.

Discussion

Suggestions are given for the main points to be discussed before, during and after the activity. These are given for guidance only and are not supposed to be rigidly followed. The children will no doubt have their own unique ideas and observations which will inspire many alternative interesting discussions! During the activity, remember to encourage children to review and modify their work as it progresses. Teachers will need to do this sensitively only when they feel it appropriate for individual children.

Evaluation

Once the art work has been displayed, it is important to evaluate the activity. Children need help to talk about both the successful and unsuccessful aspects of their own work and to see how other children in the class tackled the same problem. Comparing and contrasting different outcomes to the same task can be very beneficial. It is only by encouraging sensitive discussion of their own and others' work that children will develop a critical awareness of art and an ability to form and articulate opinions about it.

Follow-up

Art has many natural links with other areas of the curriculum and the suggestions given in this section show how the art activity can be developed and extended both within the art curriculum and in other subjects which are given in brackets.

Line

Chapter one

Early years pupils are often most familiar with this 'art element'. Usually, their first mark-making experiences have been with a pencil or crayon, creating random scribbled lines on paper. Initially, the lines simply reflect the way in which their hand has moved over the paper. Gradually, young children develop increased control over these lines and their marks become more purposeful.

With improving co-ordination skills and developing intellectual abilities, they begin to use lines deliberately to form shapes which they can name and which represent familiar people or objects in their lives. The same lines and shapes are often repeated and the child develops a range of personal marks, often referred to as 'schema'. As the child matures, the 'schema' become more complex, using very sophisticated marks and lines to communicate a wealth of ideas and feelings. (See diagram on page 14 for stages of development.)

Teaching strategies

The type of task offered to young children will depend heavily upon their stage of development. Children who are at the 'random scribble' stage benefit most from tasks which allow them to experiment freely in a variety of media (felt-tipped pens, pencils, crayons, pens, paint) and on different surfaces (a range of paper and card which includes different colour and textures). Lines can also be explored in three-dimensional media such as clay, Plasticine, pipe-cleaners, strips of card, string, wool or art straws.

Experienced early years teachers devise various strategies for reinforcing colour in many areas of the curriculum and line can be treated in the same way. Remember not to limit children's experiences of line to the traditional drawing media and tools suggested above. Incidental opportunities may also arise while children are using their fingers or tools (rakes, lollipop sticks, spoons) in the sand or water tray.

Look for opportunities to notice different lines in their immediate environment, both natural and man-made — on a collection of shells, on doors and windows, on cassette players or shoes. Even less obvious curriculum areas such as PE can offer incidental reinforcement. Can the children walk, skip or jog to make a straight or curved pathway?

Talk about the similarities or differences in the lines they are creating. This will introduce them to the essential vocabulary (straight, curved, wiggly, zigzag, thick, thin, long, short, dotted) which they will need to describe not only their own work but that of other people.

Once children have developed recognisable 'schema', more structured tasks can be presented to them. There is no need to devise artificial exercises which are isolated from the rest of the curriculum. Find opportunities to focus on this concept within the everyday tasks you would normally present to pupils. The easiest aspect of line to present first of all is the idea of long and short lines. This can form an integral part of many everyday activities from lining up for assembly to handwriting patterns as well as being the focus of a specific art activity such as drawing hands (see page 20). Go on to explore the concept of thick and thin lines in a range of media from pencil to paint and from pastels to play dough. If children are being asked to draw Dr Foster in a giant puddle, why not explore thick and thin lines in the concentric rings of the puddle? Similarly, look for ways to focus on another basic concept — straight and curved lines. When drawing imaginary maps or playing with train sets or road systems, suggest the children think about whether their roads, rivers, railway tracks and so on will be curved or straight.

Many young children are capable of exploring more complex ideas about line. Assignments can be set which increase their awareness of how lines are used to create shapes, patterns and textures.

Children can also be introduced to using lines to create dark or light areas by varying the pressure they put on media such as pencils, coloured pencils, wax crayons, charcoal and chalks.

Similarly, they can be shown how to 'soften' hard distinct lines by smudging (as with charcoal, chalks or oil pastels) or adding water (to drawings in pen or felt-tipped pens).

Even more abstract ideas such as the 'expressive' use of line to portray movement can be touched upon so long as it links naturally to work already being undertaken. The difference between continuous and broken or dotted lines can be introduced if related to the environment (such as road markings) or to studying examples of the work of others (such as Aboriginal paintings — see page 30).

At the end of this chapter, two activities are suggested which show how it is possible to link a focus on line directly to specific artists (William Morris and Maurice Sendak). Before undertaking these activities, it would be wiser for the children to have experienced some of the previous activities so they already have the necessary knowledge and language. For example, the activity based on the work of William Morris presumes the children can identify long/short, thick/thin, curved/straight lines. To gain the maximum benefit from looking at Maurice Sendak's work, the children would also need to understand how line can be used to create textures and tone.

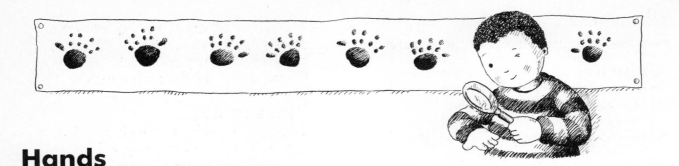

Hands

Objective
To learn the difference between long and short lines by drawing hands from observation.

What you need
Pale coloured sugar paper in two sizes, charcoal, fixative, magnifying glasses.

Preparation
Encourage the children to look closely at their hands. Name the various parts (wrist, thumb, knuckles, fingers, nails, palm and so on.) and explore their possible movements. Why are these movements useful? Discuss the relative sizes of the thumb and fingers. Ask the children to look carefully at the lines on their hands. Where can long and short lines be found both on the palm and the back of the hand? Allow the children ample time to use magnifying glasses to examine more closely.

What to do
Explain to the children that they are going to draw their hand from observation. They can draw either the palm or the back of their hand. Encourage them to observe the hand they are not using to work with.

Allow them to choose the colour and size of their paper and emphasise that their drawing should fill the space. Discuss the problems of accidental smudging with the charcoal and how to avoid this. Once they have drawn the basic shape of their hand, ask them to show as many of the lines on their hand as possible.

When the drawings are finished, spray them with fixative following the manufacturer's instructions.

Discussion
While they work, talk with the children about their drawing. Remind them to keep looking closely at their hand. Have they drawn the right number of fingers? Can you see the nails and the wrist? Ask them to point out where they have used long and short lines. Encourage more mature children to consider whether they could add more detail.

Evaluation
Talk with the children about the results, comparing and contrasting the drawings of different children. Which hand shows the fingers in the most interesting pose? Can they point to examples of long and short lines in the drawings? Has any child used mostly long lines or mostly short lines? Do these appear on any particular part of the hand, such as the fingers?

Follow-up
Use an inking pad to take each child's fingerprints. Compare and contrast the lines on them. Are any two children's fingerprints the same? (Science)

Houses

Objective
To learn to distinguish between thick and thin lines using play dough.

What you need
Coloured sugar paper, play dough, modelling tools, pencils, cartridge paper.

Preparation
Take the children to look at several different houses and, if feasible, ask them to draw one of the houses from observation. Try to move away from the stereotyped square with triangle roof by focusing their attention on the shape and position of the real roof, doors and windows. Encourage them to include details such as drainpipes, guttering, tiles and special features (porches, balconies). If the children have drawn real houses, they will find the following task much easier and will produce work of greater quality.

Show the children how to roll out coils of play dough to make lines. Deliberately make some of the coils thick and some thin so as to introduce this concept.

What to do
Display the children's pencil drawings of houses close to where they will be working. Explain that they are going to use their drawing of a house to inspire a play dough relief (a sculpture cut into or built up on a flat surface — see Figure 1). They will also need to think about using the play dough to make thick and thin lines in their relief.

Ask them to choose a piece of coloured sugar paper on which to place their play dough relief. Once they have made their house with play dough, suggest they use the modelling tools to scratch thick and thin lines into some of the play dough. For example, they may wish to put lines on to the door or chimney. When the reliefs are dry, display them with the pencil drawings of houses which inspired the activity.

sugar paper

coils of play dough placed on paper to make picture of house

texture added to coils and slabs of play dough

Figure 1

Discussion

While they are working, refer them back to their original pencil drawings for ideas and to remind them of details. What happens as they roll the coils? How can they turn a thick coil into a thin one? Which modelling tools make thick or thin lines?

Evaluation

Discuss the final display. How has the play dough changed as it has dried out? Can the children find thick and thin lines on several of the houses? Match the modelling tools to the thick and thin lines which have been scratched into the play dough. Which tool makes the thickest/ thinnest line? Which houses include details such as downpipes, porches or unusual shaped windows? Is it possible to match the original pencil drawings to any of the play dough houses? Which house would the children most like to live in and why?

Follow-up

Try using other plastic materials (clay, Plasticine, pastry) to make reliefs using thick and thin lines. Compare the similarities and differences between each material. (Science)

Wool collage

Objective

To learn the differences between straight and curved lines.

What you need

Pipe-cleaners, Multilink cubes (including triangular prism pieces), a model railway track, a collection of toy cars, different coloured sugar paper in three sizes, PVA adhesive, glue sticks, scissors, a variety of wool (different colours, thicknesses, textures).

Preparation

Show the children several straight pipe-cleaners and ask them to find objects in the room which have straight lines on them. Then bend the pipe-cleaners into different curved lines and ask them to find objects which have curved lines on them. Discuss their examples.

Ask the children to make curved and straight lines with appropriate materials in the classroom. For example, can they place the toy cars in a straight line? Can they make a curved line with the Multilink cubes and triangular prisms? Can they sort the railway track into sets of straight or curved pieces?

What to do

Ask each child to choose a piece of coloured sugar paper and cover one side with PVA adhesive. Invite them to make straight or curved lines by pressing the wool on to the adhesive. Encourage

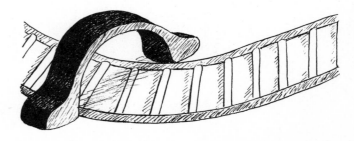

those who have grasped the idea of curved and straight lines, to select wools in a variety of colours, textures and thicknesses. Adult assistance may be needed to cut the wool.

Discussion
Ask each child to describe the sugar paper they have chosen – a small red piece or a medium sized blue piece. Talk about the lines they have created with the wool. Which lines are straight and which are curved? Does one line wiggle more than any of the others? Do they prefer curved lines to straight lines?

For children who have understood the differences between curved and straight lines, use this opportunity to reinforce the concepts from the previous activities on long/short and thick/thin lines.

Evaluation
Once the pictures are displayed, ask one or two children to talk about their pictures. Can they point to the curved or straight lines in their picture? Has anyone used a lot more curved lines than straight ones? Do any of the pictures remind the children of something?

Follow-up
Allow the children to play with a collection of pipe-cleaners, exploring the idea of straight and curved lines. Can they make a picture or model with them? Is it possible to join the pipe-cleaners together? (Art)

Bicycles

Objective
To learn that lines can be used to create shapes.

What you need
A child's bicycle, a chalkboard, chalk, white cartridge paper, soft pencils (6B).

Preparation
Discuss the child's bicycle, naming the various parts of it and drawing attention to their shape. As each plane shape (square, circle, triangle, oblong) is identified, ask a child to draw that shape on the chalkboard. Talk about how many lines are needed to draw each shape and their relative sizes.

What to do
Explain to the children that they are going to draw the bicycle from observation. Ask them to decide whether they need their paper in the landscape or portrait position. Remind them to make their drawing fill the whole of the paper. Invite them to use lines to draw the main shapes which they can see on the bicycle. Display the completed drawings near to the bicycle.

Discussion
Encourage the children to refer back to the bicycle for details. Talk about the shapes they are drawing and how they join together to form a picture of the bicycle. If the children have previous experience of long/short, thick/thin, straight/curved lines, extend the discussion to include references to these.

Evaluation
Compare and contrast the finished drawings. Talk about the shapes which appear in the drawings. Can the children find examples of each of the plane shapes (triangle, circle, square, oblong) on the bicycle drawings? Ask one or two children to describe how many straight or curved lines are needed to draw the shape. Count how many circles can be found on one or two of the drawings. For which part of the bicycles have triangles been drawn?

Follow-up
Use finger paints to draw plane shapes on to coloured sugar paper. Invite the children to use the finger paints to colour in some of the plane shapes they have drawn. Extend the idea of shapes in isolation, by asking more mature children to make some of the shapes touch or overlap so that they create new shapes.
(Art)

Teddy bears

Objective
To use lines to record the texture on a teddy bear.

What you need
Beige or sandy coloured sugar paper in two different sizes, small pieces of scrap paper, charcoal, fixative, a collection of teddy bears.

Preparation
Allow the children time to handle the teddy bears before this activity. Choose one of the bears and talk with the children about it in detail. Count and name the body parts. Discuss the bear's colour, shape, size and any distinguishing features. Draw the children's attention to the bear's texture. Is the fur short or long? Does it cover the whole body or only part? Ask the children to close their eyes and feel the rough and smooth areas on the teddy bear.

What to do
Ask the children to choose a teddy bear and use the charcoal to draw a large picture of it from observation. Allow them to choose the size of their paper and discuss whether they will use it in the portrait or landscape position. Remind them to take care not to lean on their work accidentally.

As the children draw, ask them to think about how they are going to show the texture of the fur. What kind of lines will they use for the rough and smooth areas on their teddy? If the children are experienced in using charcoal, show them how to achieve a soft, fluffy effect by smudging with a finger or paper tissue and invite them to use this technique.

Spray the finished drawings with fixative following the manufacturer's instructions and display them with the collection of teddy bears.

Discussion

While they work, encourage the children to look carefully at their teddy and include all the body parts. Have they forgotten his ears or nose? Did they remember any special features such as a bow or hat?

Talk with them about the lines they are using to represent the fur. Are they straight, curved, long, short, thick or thin? Encourage them to think carefully before smudging any lines. Are they going to smudge all the lines representing fur or only some of them? Will they smudge by moving their finger in the same direction as the line or by smudging across it? If they are not sure, allow them to experiment on some scrap paper.

Evaluation

Discuss the children's drawings, focusing particularly upon the various kinds of lines they have used to create texture. Compare two or three drawings which use very different lines to represent fur. For example, one child may have used short straight lines whilst another may have used long curved lines. Can the children point to lines which have been smudged in the pictures? Which teddy bear appears to be the softest? Can they match any of the drawings to the real teddy bears? Which teddy bear would they most like to cuddle and why?

Follow-up

Ask the children to choose a teddy bear and invent a family for it. Does it have a wife, mother, granny, son or uncle? Suggest they choose their own medium and draw a picture of the bear and its family and write about them. (Art and English)

Snails

Objective

To use lines to record the patterns found on snails.

What you need

A collection of snails, white cartridge paper in two different sizes, soft pencils (6B), magnifying glasses.

Preparation

Allow the children time to handle and observe the snails using magnifying glasses. Talk with them about their observations. Can they name the various body parts? How does the snail move or feed? What colours can be found on them? Are they familiar with the spiral shape on the shell? What other spiral shapes do they know about? Can they draw a spiral shape in the air? Draw their attention particularly to the patterns found on the shell. What kind of lines can be found in these patterns?

What to do

Explain to the children that they are going to use a pencil to draw a snail from observation and allow them to choose the size of their paper. Remind them that their picture should almost fill the paper. Emphasise that they should pay particular attention to the lines which form the patterns on the shell and the soft body. Be careful when handling the snails and don't forget to return them to their natural habitat.

Discussion

While they draw, refer them back to the real snails for details. Talk about the various lines they are using. Are they drawing a straight or curved line? Where have they drawn long or short lines? Will they want to make some of the lines thick? Which lines are they repeating to form a pattern? Can they describe the pattern on the shell?

Evaluation

Compare and contrast the lines used by the children to show the patterns on the snails. Have any of them used the same kind of lines? Has anyone found more unusual lines to represent the pattern? Look at two or three very different drawings and encourage the children to identify the lines which have been repeated to form a pattern.

Follow-up

Extend the above activity by using the drawings from observation to inspire work from imagination. Invite the children to use felt-tipped pens to draw an imaginary snail with an interesting pattern. (Art)

Kettles

Objective

To use lines to record the tone (light and dark areas) on a kettle.

What you need

A collection of metallic kettles, two or three examples of pencil drawings which contain obvious contrasts in tone (these could be drawings by older pupils in the school, secondary school pupils, a local artist, a famous historical or contemporary artist), white cartridge paper in two different sizes, pencils (6B).

Preparation

Show the children the kettles and make sure they understand the vocabulary for naming various parts of the kettle (spout, handle, lid, flex, plug). Compare the various designs, highlighting similarities and differences in shape, colour, size and materials. Then ask the children to identify first the dark areas and then the light areas on one of the kettles. Compare their findings with a second kettle. Are the dark and light areas the same?

Encourage the children to look carefully at the examples of pencil drawings and to identify the light and dark areas in them. Can they suggest how the artists achieved this? Demonstrate on a piece of paper how dark lines can be created by pressing hard with a pencil and light lines by pressing gently.

What to do

Explain to the children that they are going to draw one of the kettles. Allow them to choose the kettle and the size of their paper. Encourage the children to think about the most suitable position for the paper (landscape or portrait). Ask them to look carefully at the kettle and use the pencil to draw the main shapes they can see. Remind them to fill the paper with their drawing and refer them back to the kettle for details. Once they have drawn the main shapes of their kettle, suggest they try shading some areas in their drawing.

Display the collection of kettles with the final drawings.

Discussion

As the children draw, ask them to name the various parts of their kettle and to think about whether they have included all the details. Very young children may not necessarily be able to match exactly the dark areas on their drawing to the dark areas on the kettle but it is still useful for them to practise varying the pressure on their pencil to create a variety of tone.

Evaluation

Compare and contrast the finished drawings. Can the children identify the dark and light lines in some of the drawings? Which is the darkest/lightest part? Is it possible to match any of the drawings to the real kettles? Which children have managed to match most accurately the dark and light lines in their drawing to their kettle?

Follow-up

Allow the children to experiment with various grades of pencil (try HB, 2B and 6B) to find out any differences in the shading they can produce. Which pencil makes the darkest/lightest lines? (Art)

Feathers

Objective

To learn how hard, distinct pen lines can be softened with water.

What you need

A collection of feathers, black pens, white cartridge paper in two different sizes, scrap paper, water pots, small brushes, magnifying glasses.

Preparation
Allow the children time to handle the feathers and examine them with the magnifying glasses. Compare and contrast several different feathers. What colour, shape or size are they? How do they feel? Which areas are hard or soft? Do they have the same markings all over? What kinds of line can the children see on them?

What to do
Ask the children to choose a feather to draw from observation. Invite them to choose the size of their paper and decide in which position they are going to place both the paper and the feather. Challenge the children to use the pens to draw a large picture of the feather showing all the different lines they can see. They may wish to continue using the magnifying glasses as an aid. Once they have finished drawing, it may be appropriate for them to use the pens to colour some dark areas on their feather so as to show any dark markings or spots.

On some scrap paper, show them how to use the brush to apply a small amount of water on top of the pen lines or markings. What effect does this have? Suggest they might like to use this method to show which lines or areas are softer.

Display the feathers with the final drawings.

Discussion
As they draw, talk with the children about their feather, encouraging them to include as many details as possible. Discuss the various kinds of line they are using and which areas they feel need to be darkened by colouring in.

Invite them to experiment with adding water to a drawing on some scrap paper before applying it to their own drawing. Can they describe what happens when a small amount of water is applied both to ordinary lines and to a very dark area? What if too much water is added? Encourage them to be selective when adding the water. Which areas need to be softened with the water and which would be better left as they are?

Evaluation
Choose one or two drawings and ask the children to describe all the different types of line which have been used to draw the feathers (long/short, thick/thin, straight/curved). Compare and contrast the lines which have been softened by water with those which have not. Can the children think of a different subject matter which would benefit from this technique?

Follow-up
Try using felt-tipped pens to draw a rainy day picture on blotting paper. Paint over selected areas with water and compare the effects achieved with the black pens. (Art)

Water

Objective
To explore how lines can be used to create the impression of movement on water.

What you need
Blue card cut into oblongs of different sizes, PVA adhesive, glue sticks, thick string, scissors, printing trays, printing ink (blue, green, purple), printing rollers, white cartridge or pale blue sugar paper approximately the same size as the card.

Preparation
Take the children to look at a pond and observe the lines created by the movement of the water. If a pond is not available, use a large puddle or a water tray. Change the movement of the water by throwing in a pebble or stirring it with a stick. (This is best done by an adult if the water is very deep). Encourage the children to notice the difference in the lines when the water is calm and when it is moving. Collect pictures or photographs of water as it appears in lakes, rivers, seas, streams and so on. Encourage the children to describe the lines they can see in the photographs.

If the children have no experience of using printing rollers, allow them a period of free play with the printing inks and some spare pieces of sugar or cartridge paper.

What to do
Allow the children to choose a piece of blue card and decide in which position to place it before starting. Explain that they are going to build up a printing block. The string is going to represent the lines on the surface of water and they must show whether their water is calm or rough and stormy. Ask them to cover one side of their piece of card with PVA adhesive and then press pieces of string on to the adhesive. (They may need help to cut the string.) Allow the printing blocks to dry overnight or even longer if necessary. Place the blue printing ink in a printing tray and show the children how to get the ink on to the roller by rolling it backwards and forwards in the tray. Invite them to use the roller to cover all the string on their block with blue ink. Remind them to clean their hands before choosing the correct sized cartridge or sugar paper to place on top of their block. Very young children may need help in placing the paper correctly. Use a clean roller to press firmly over the back of the cartridge or sugar paper so as to transfer the image from the string to the paper. Peel the paper off carefully and allow the print to dry.

In order to create a more complex arrangement of lines, repeat the above process. Use the same colour or try a second colour (such as green or purple) on top of the original blue image. The use of two colours can add to the sense of movement. Allow the children to choose how they place the paper and do not worry about achieving an exact 'register' (that is, placing the paper in the same position as for the previous print). In fact, more complex images result if the paper has been rotated before printing.

Discussion
As they press the string into the adhesive, talk about the lines the string is making. Are they long, short, curved or straight? Encourage them to persevere until the whole of their block has interesting lines on it. Are there any large empty spaces? Are they trying to create the impression of rough or calm water? Remind them of their observations of real water.

As they are printing, encourage them to talk about what is happening. Is it easy to load the roller evenly with ink? What happens if you have a large blob of ink in the middle of the inking tray or use the roller too quickly? Does one coat of ink with the roller cover all the string? How many coats are needed before all the string is covered? Why is this important? What will happen if some of the string is left bare? Talk about the need for using a clean roller when pressing on the back. Also discuss why it is important not to move the paper on the block while printing. Before applying the second colour, talk about the results achieved by using just one colour.

Evaluation
It might be useful to show the whole process by displaying an original block, a single blue print and then a second print with two colours. Can the children help describe the whole printing process.

What were the difficulties and points to remember for the future? Which prints make them think of calm or rough and stormy water? What kind of lines have been used to create this impression? Which print do they like best and why?

Follow-up
Write a class poem with two verses, one about rough water and one about calm water. Use their observations of real water, photographs and their string prints as inspiration. (English)

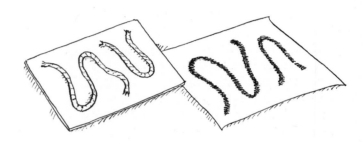

Aboriginal paintings

Objective
To learn the differences between dotted and continuous lines through a study of Aboriginal paintings.

What you need
Examples of Aboriginal paintings (look on greetings cards, postcards, calendars and books such as *Dreamings* by Peter Sutton (Viking, Penguin Books Australia), terracotta coloured sugar paper in two sizes, paint (black, yellow, white, brown), palettes, water pots, a collection of twigs.

Preparation
Discuss the examples of Aboriginal paintings with the children. Explain that the original paintings would probably have been painted on bark using twigs.

Compare the examples and look for similarities in subject matter (often wildlife, such as lizards, snakes, turtles) and colours (usually white, black, yellow, brown). Then ask the children to describe the different types of line used in the paintings. As well as looking for various aspects of line covered in previous activities (long/short, thick/thin, curved/straight), a striking feature of many Aboriginal paintings is the use of dotted lines. Can the children find examples in the paintings of these? Where have long continuous lines been used?

Invite the children to make a collection of twigs to use to paint with.

What to do

Explain to the children that they are going to paint their own version of an Aboriginal painting based on the examples they have seen. They do not need to try to copy one of the paintings exactly but can incorporate any aspect of the Aboriginal paintings into their picture. Encourage them to use both dotted and continuous lines.

Allow them to choose the size of their paper and decide which position to place it in (landscape or portrait). Encourage them to use a variety of twigs to paint their picture — they may need a piece of scrap paper to experiment on. Remind them to wash the twig before changing colours.

Display the final paintings with the original examples of Aboriginal paintings.

Discussion

As the children paint, talk with them about the different kinds of line they are using. Are they making a curved or straight dotted line? Is their continuous line thick or thin? Do different twigs produce different lines? Is it easier to make a dotted or continuous line with a twig?

Evaluation

Discuss the final paintings and ask the children to find similarities between their own paintings and the Aboriginal examples. Focus particularly upon examples of dotted and continuous lines.

Follow-up

Find out more about Aboriginal culture and make a class book about the children's discoveries. (Geography)

Plants

Objective
To link examples of William Morris' work based on plants to the children's experiences of line.

What you need
Examples of work based on plants by William Morris — these can be found on fabrics, wallpaper, wrapping paper, stationery. Press-print titles (special polystyrene blocks available from art suppliers), pencils, printing ink (limited to one dark colour), printing trays, rollers, pieces of cartridge or sugar paper (a pale colour) large enough to allow several prints for each press-print tile.

Preparation
Discuss the examples of work by William Morris, focusing on the shape and colour of the plants. How many different types of plant have been used? Is there a repeating pattern? Name the various parts of a plant and identify which parts are used in each example. Concentrate specifically on the different types of line which which feature in each example. Are they long, short, straight, curved, thick or thin? Which example do the children like best and why?

If they are unfamiliar with the use of printing rollers, allow them a period of play to experiment with them.

What to do
Explain to the children that they are going to print their own wallpaper based on William Morris' work. Give each child a piece of press-print tile (one tile can be cut into several pieces) and ask them to use a pencil to draw a similar plant design on their tile. Encourage them to press firmly to make an indent but not so hard that they go through the tile.

Remind them how to use the roller to apply the ink to the tile. When the tile is covered with ink, turn it upside down and place it on one corner of the cartridge or sugar paper. Very young children may need help to place the tile on to the paper. Use a clean roller to press firmly on the back of the tile to transfer the print on to the paper. Peel off the tile to reveal the print. Repeat the above process, placing each print adjacent to the previous one until the whole paper is covered.

Discussion
Talk with the children while they draw their plant designs on to their tile. Refer them back to the original Morris examples for ideas. Are they going to include leaves and buds in their design? Will the stems be long and curved? What shape and size will the flowers be? What kind of lines have they used? Encourage them to cover most of their tile with drawings and not to leave too many large empty spaces.

While they are printing, encourage them to describe what is happening. Is the whole of the tile covered in ink? What will happen if it is not? Why do we need to press firmly on the back of the tile? What will happen if the paper is moved while printing?

Evaluation
First compare and contrast the lines used on two or three of the children's examples and then relate these to the original Morris samples. Then ask the children to help describe the process they used and discuss any difficulties they encountered. Talk about the quality of prints on one example. Are some prints clearer than others? Can the children explain this? Have the prints been placed well on the paper or are there large empty gaps?

Follow-up
Make a collection of wallpaper samples and use them for sorting activities — flowers/not flowers, textured/not textured, like/dislike. Invite the children to choose a favourite sample and draw their own bedroom with this particular wallpaper pattern. (Maths and Art)

Dreams

Objective
To link illustrations by Maurice Sendak to the children's experiences of line.

What you need
A copy of the book *Where the Wild Things Are* by Maurice Sendak (Picture Puffin), writing paper, pencils, white cartridge paper, black pens, coloured pencils, coloured sugar paper, adhesive, stapler. (This activity could be adapted to any illustrator — for example, Pat Hutchins or Charles Keeping — who uses line in a dominant way.)

Preparation
Read the story to the children and ask them to write their own story about a dream. Explain that they are going to draw the illustrations after they have written the story. When they have finished the story, suggest they divide the text up, deciding where illustrations would be appropriate. Ask them to write the final version of the text on separate pieces of paper which can later be mounted with the illustrations. If the children have not yet developed the writing skills necessary they could work together or the teacher could act as scribe.

Return to the book and look more closely at the illustrations. Focus on the way in which Maurice Sendak uses a wide variety of line to show the texture on the monsters' fur, hair and tails. Encourage the children to identify the light and dark areas in one or two illustrations and discuss how this has been achieved (by placing the pen lines close together or far apart and by cross-hatching (see Figure 1). Demonstrate these effects on paper using a black pen.

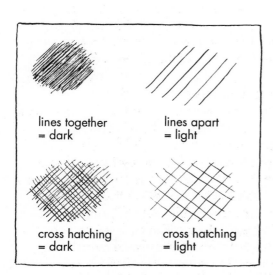

lines together = dark

lines apart = light

cross hatching = dark

cross hatching = light

Figure 1

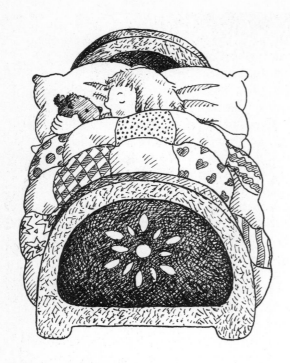

What to do

Give the children the black pens and white cartridge paper. Ask them to draw pictures to illustrate the text of their story. This may need to be spread over several days. Refer the children back to the book illustrations for ideas. Encourage them to use a wide variety of lines to create texture in their illustrations. More mature children may also be capable of trying out the two methods to depict tone (light and dark). When the children have finished their pen drawings, invite them to add colour to their illustrations using the coloured pencils. Once again, they could try to use different kinds of line to create texture and tone.

Mount the finished illustrations with the text on coloured sugar paper to make a book. Display the original story book with the children's stories about dreams.

Discussion

As the children draw, talk with them about the kind of lines they are using (long/short, thick/thin, straight/curved).

What type of lines have they used to show the texture of an animal's fur or a person's hair? Could they improve an area of their drawing by adding lines to show the texture of grass, tree bark or fabrics? Would short spiky lines be more appropriate than long wavy ones? Encourage more mature children to look for opportunities in their drawings to create light or dark areas. Is it possible to make one animal's tail dark by drawing lots of lines close together? Would cross-hatching add shadows to tree trunks or buildings?

Remind the children to continue thinking about using lines to depict texture and tone when using their coloured pencils. When adding colour to an animal's fur, can the children use the same kind of lines as they did with the black pen? As well as cross-hatching and the spacing of lines, tone can also be created by changing the pressure used on the coloured pencils. Encourage the children to try pressing gently to produce light colours and firmly to produce dark.

Evaluation

At storytime each day, invite the children to read their stories to the class. Discuss the stories and illustrations. Ask the children to identify textures in the pictures and describe what kind of line has been used. Can they point to light and dark areas in an illustration and say how the effect was achieved? Compare the illustrations in one or two of the children's books with Maurice Sendak's. What are the similarities and differences? Which illustrations do the children prefer?

Follow-up

Invite the children to read each other's stories and then write a book review about one which they particularly enjoyed. Encourage them to write comments about the illustrations as well as the text. (English)

Shape

Chapter two

Shape is a popular theme to explore with early years pupils. Many children are taught to recognise and name both plane shapes (circle, square, oblong, triangle, hexagon) and three-dimensional shapes (cylinder, cube, cuboid, sphere, triangular prism, cone, pyramid, hexagonal prism). Obviously, there are strong cross-curricular links with mathematics.

Teaching strategies

Shapes are all around us so there is no shortage of resources to study. Focus on shapes in nature (insects, stones, trees) as well as those in the man-made environment (toys, buildings, furniture). Children can become aware of shapes incidentally through their play with puzzles, mosaics and bricks. Offer them a range of construction kits (Duplo, Reo-Click, Mobilo) so they have opportunities to build with as many different shaped materials as possible. More structured activities, such as sorting or shape matching games, can provide valuable ways of reinforcing both the shape names and other relevant vocabulary, such as edge, curved, straight and corners.

Early on in the development of their drawings, children begin consciously to use lines to draw shapes. Circles are usually the most common recognisable shape to appear first. Many of their initial 'schema' (personal symbols repeatedly used to represent familiar objects or people) are a combination of simple shapes and can be reinforced through discussion. What shape are they going to use to draw a bus? How many circles have they used to draw their mum's face? Which shape would make a good chimney on their model of a house?

Adult artists often deliberately manipulate shape to convey their feelings and ideas both within the composition of two-dimensional work and the construction of three-dimensional work. For example, an artist may be consciously emphasising triangle shapes in a landscape to convey his own emotional response to it. Similarly, a sculptress may be very interested in representing the rounded, organic forms she sees in tree roots. In both cases, an

understanding of shape would be crucial to the artist's success in communicating with the viewer. No-one would expect young children to use shapes in such a sophisticated manner, but it is possible to set them on their way.

Initially, offer activities which will help them learn to name shapes and become aware of characteristics, such as the number and shape of their faces (3D shapes) and edges (2D shapes). Activities such as Robots (p37) and Doors and windows (p41) will provide opportunities to introduce and reinforce knowledge about shapes.

Once they can recognise and name shapes, it is useful to set assignments which focus attention on one particular aspect of shape. With three-dimensional shapes, children will need to experience tasks which involve joining a variety of materials together to create a new three-dimensional shape (using boxes, card or other materials). It is also important to offer tasks which require them to create a three-dimensional shape by removing materials (carving into play dough, Plasticine or clay).

Activities which involve matching objects (or pictures of objects) to silhouette shapes will introduce the idea that many things are easily identifiable purely by their overall shape. Repeating shapes to form patterns is a popular mathematical activity and is often introduced via mosaics or beads. This is an important concept in art and can be reinforced through a whole host of activities. Similarly, distinguishing between shapes with curved or straight edges is another mathematical skill which is invaluable to the artist.

Many young children are also capable of understanding that shapes can be joined, divided or overlapped to create new shapes. It is important for children to develop the confidence to experiment with shapes in this way. Activities (such as Fruit, p47) which encourage children to play with shape help them realise that often there are several solutions to an art activity and their first idea is not always the most appropriate. More complex concepts can be introduced to more mature children. For example, some children can appreciate that the shape of something changes if viewed from a different direction and this is an important concept not only for art but also for developing geographical mapping skills.

Similarly, it is possible to encourage children to look at the shapes in between objects and so begin to introduce the idea of positive shapes (the objects) and negative shapes (the space surrounding the objects) (see Figure 1).

Two activities at the end of the chapter show how early years pupils can begin to appreciate that shape plays an important part in the work of well-known artists such as Barbara Hepworth and Gustav Klimt. Before attempting these children will need to be able to recognise both two and three-dimensional shapes and patterns and overlapping shapes.

Robots

Objective
To recognise solid shapes and their faces.

What you need
A collection of toy robots, a large number of materials such as boxes, packets and tubes (to include examples of as many different solid shapes as possible), brightly coloured sugar paper, PVA adhesive, glue sticks, scissors, paper fasteners, felt-tipped pens, pencils.

Preparation
Discuss the collection of toy robots. Do they have faces, arms, legs, tails? How do they move? Compare and contrast their colour, texture and the materials they are made from. Focus particularly upon the solid shapes to be found in each one. Can the children find a similar shape in the collection of materials?

What to do
Invite the children to choose a shape (box or packet) for the main part of their robot's body. Allow them to choose a piece of coloured sugar paper and show them how to draw round each face of

negative shapes positive shapes

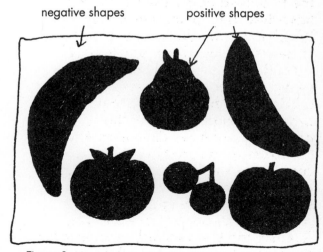

Figure 1

their shape. They can then cut out the shapes and stick them on to their box or packet. Repeat this process with a smaller box or packet if they want to add another shape for the head.

Encourage them to add features to their robot by cutting and sticking different coloured sugar paper to make antennae, eyes, arms, buttons and dials. Show them how to use a paper fastener to make a dial or lever which moves (see Figure 1).

Allow the robots to dry and then use the felt-tipped pens to add any patterns or textures. Display the model robots alongside the toy ones.

Discussion
While the children work, talk with them about the solid shapes they have each chosen. What are they called? How many faces will they have to draw round? What shape are the faces? Refer them back to the toy robots for ideas on what other features to include.

Evaluation
Discuss the display of robots. Choose two or three robots and ask the children to name the solid shapes which have been used and identify their various faces. Which robot has used the most cylinders or cubes? Do all the cuboids have the same shaped faces? Can anyone explain the various features on their robot and how it moves? What do the buttons and levers do? Which robot do they like best and why?

Follow-up
Ask the children to draw and colour their robot model from different viewpoints, labelling the materials used in the construction. (Technology)

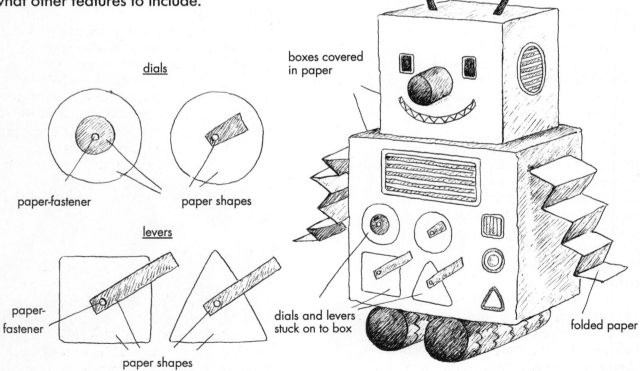

dials

paper-fastener   paper shapes

levers

paper-fastener

paper shapes

boxes covered in paper

dials and levers stuck on to box

folded paper

Figure 1

38

Machines

Objectives
To explore how new three-dimensional shapes can be created by joining other shapes together.

What you need
Brightly coloured card cut into plane shapes, elastic bands, paper-clips, paper-fasteners, treasury tags, string, coloured sponge cloths cut into strips, matchsticks, lollipop sticks, art straws.

Preparation
The children should be given the opportunity to observe a wide range of different machines as a stimulus for this activity. For example, show them a vacuum cleaner, computer, food processor, lawnmower or strimmer. Encourage them to notice the arrangement of buttons on control panels and particular machine parts such as wheels, cogs, levers, springs. Identify as many shapes as possible on the machines.

Show the children the materials listed above and discuss their colour, texture, material from which they are made and, in particular, their shape. If necessary, demonstrate how they can be joined to each other.

What to do
Explain to the children that they are going to join together the above materials to make an imaginary machine. They can use any of the materials they wish but they must not use adhesive to join them. It is also important that their machine has an interesting overall shape. As they work, they need to think about what function their 'machine' will perform.

When the children have finished their machines, ask each of them to show you exactly how they want their machine displayed. Some will have joined the materials to make a flat picture which may be best stapled to a display board. Others may have tried to build a more three-dimensional structure and it may be more suitable to display these on a table or display boxes. Ask each child to dictate one or two sentences describing their machine and add this as a label.

Discussion
As they work, talk with them about the shapes they are using. What shape do you get if you join two paper-clips together? How many circles will their machine have, if any? Can they fold or bend the card and sponge cloth to create a new shape? Is it possible to change the shape of the straws, string or elastic bands by knotting or tying? How are they going to join two materials together? What is their machine called and what does it do?

Evaluation
Discuss the finished display, initially focusing on the name and function of each machine. Then talk about the materials which have been used in two or three examples and ask the children to describe what they did. Did any of them create new shapes by folding, bending, knotting or tying? Ask the children to

describe the shapes in the machines. Which plane shapes can they see? Have any solid shapes such as a cylinder been created? Can they see any shapes which have been joined to create a totally new shape? Which machine do they like best and why?

Follow-up
Allow the children to work in groups to arrange a small collection of PE apparatus to create an interesting overall layout for movement activities. Try using hoops, ropes, mats, benches, bean bags, quoits and planks. What individual shapes have they used and what shape do the apparatus form when joined? Ask the children to demonstrate how their layout would be used and suggest a variety of alternative movements. (PE)

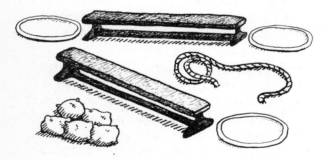

Towers

Objective
To explore how new three-dimensional shapes can be created by carving.

What you need
A story such as Rapunzel which refers to a tower, a collection of pictures of different towers (multicultural, historical and contemporary), small blocks of leather hard clay (see Preparation), modelling tools including wire-ended tools, wooden boards or ceramic tiles to stand the clay on while working.

Preparation
Leather hard (sometimes called cheese hard) clay is achieved by allowing the blocks of clay to dry out until they are stiff but still damp enough to carve into. This process may take a day or two depending upon the water content of the clay and the room temperature. Encourage the children to compare the feel of the clay both before and after it dries.

Read the story of Rapunzel to the children and show them the pictures of towers. Focus particularly upon the various shapes. Which ones are shaped like a cylinder or a cuboid? Do any have unusual shapes such as a triangular prism or hexagonal prism? Are the towers the same shape all the way up or does the shape alter at the top? Discuss the shape of any features such as doors, windows, staircases or decoration.

If the children are unfamiliar with the modelling tools and the wire-ended tools, demonstrate how to use them to carve into a piece of clay.

What to do
Explain to the children that they are going to make an imaginary tower like the one in the story. Give them a small block of clay and ask them to stand it on a wooden board or ceramic tile. Suggest they start by carving the overall shape and refer them back to the pictures for ideas. Then ask them to carve out features such as doors, windows or staircases. Finally, invite them to add patterns or textures to their tower by carving or scratching into the clay with the modelling tools. If the towers are to be fired, they may need to be hollowed out and adult assistance may be required. Leave the finished towers to dry out before firing. Display the completed towers alongside the pictures and story that inspired the activity.

Discussion

Talk with the children about the overall shape of their tower, encouraging them to consider more unusual shapes such as triangular or hexagonal prisms. Will the top of their tower be a different shape such as cone or pyramid? Discuss the shape of the various features. Will the doors all be the same shape and size? How will the windows be arranged? What shapes are created in the decoration? Discuss the advantages and disadvantages of the various tools the children are using. Highlight the carving process by drawing their attention to the clay which has been removed.

Evaluation

Look carefully at the finished towers and compare the shapes which have been achieved. How many cylinder shapes are there? Which ones have a cone at the top? Was one shape more difficult to carve? Ask one or two children to identify any two-dimensional shapes on their tower. Have they scratched in oblong bricks or square tiles? Which tower do they like best and why?

Follow-up

Suggest the children use their towers for measuring activities. Challenge them to find five things in the classroom which are taller or shorter than their tower. Can they find a way to record their findings? (Mathematics)

Doors and windows

Objective

To encourage children to find and name plane shapes in the man-made environment.

What you need

Soft pencils (6B), white cartridge paper folded into six oblongs, small clipboards to lean on, pictures of doors and windows.

Preparation

Display a collection of pictures of doors and windows. Discuss these with the children, introducing any unfamiliar vocabulary such as door frame, hinge, letter box, window sill. Then focus on plane shapes, asking the children to point out examples of oblongs, circles, triangles and squares. Are there any other more unusual plane shapes such as hexagons?

What to do

Give each child a pencil, a piece of paper and a clipboard. Take them on a walk around the school buildings (inside and out) to study doors and windows. Explain that in each oblong space on their paper, they are going to draw a door or a window, showing all the shapes they can see. Ask them to make sure each door or window is a different design. Suggest they consider adding dark or light shading to selected areas such as the window panes, hinges or door handles. Display the children's drawing along with the pictures of doors and windows.

Discussion

Can the children guess what the clipboard is for? Give them a piece of scrap paper and let them try drawing with their paper on the ground. What are the difficulties? Look for unusual features such as frosted glass, large hinges or interesting key holes. Draw their attention to the shapes which can be seen on the doors or windows before they begin to draw. Are there any triangles? What shape are the window panes? How many circles have they drawn on their door? Which parts of their window have they chosen to shade and why?

Evaluation

Discuss the final display of drawings. Did they find any doors or windows similar in design to those in the pictures? Focus on two or three drawings and ask the children to describe the shapes. Are any of the shapes more difficult to draw? Which window had the most squares? Which door had the least circles? Which door or window did they find most or least attractive? Why?

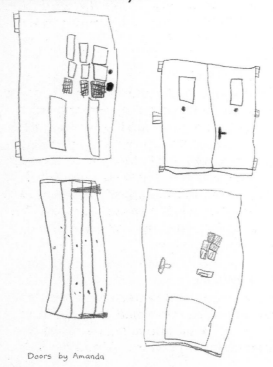

Doors by Amanda

Follow-up

Ask the children to choose one of the doors or windows which they have drawn. Suggest they use their drawing to inspire work in a medium of their choice — as a print using press-print tiles (see page 32 for details), as a sculpture using play dough or as a collage using fabric off-cuts. (Art)

Presents

Objective

To introduce the idea that shape can identify an object.

What you need

Large pictures of distinctively shaped objects or animals, black sugar paper, a collection of distinctively shaped toys (ball, teddy bear, car, aeroplane, boat and so on) wrapped in paper, white cartridge paper, pencils, wax crayons, scissors, coloured wash (yellow, blue and red), large paint brushes, a stapler, grey backing paper.

Preparation

Cut out the large pictures of objects or animals and make a black silhouette for each one by drawing round it on black sugar paper and cutting out the resulting shape. Use these for a matching game, inviting the children to match the silhouette shape to the appropriate picture. Talk about how they know which silhouette matches and help them realise that each picture has a distinctive shape.

Show them the wrapped toys and see if they can guess what is inside just by looking at the shape. If necessary, allow them to feel the presents. Unwrap each one to reveal its identity. How can they tell what the present will be just by looking at its shape?

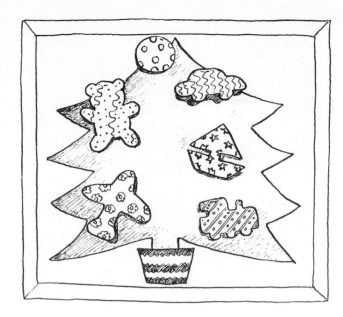

Can you guess
what presents are
hanging on our tree?

What to do

Explain to the children that they are going to draw a present and then hide it with wrapping paper so that they can play a similar guessing game.

Allow each child to choose one of the toys. Ask them to draw a large picture of it from observation, paying particular attention to the overall shape. Invite them to use the wax crayons to colour it and then cut it out. Then suggest they draw carefully round their picture of a toy on to another piece of white cartridge paper to make a white silhouette. Ask them to use the wax crayons to draw patterns on the white silhouette to make it look like wrapping paper. Help them to make sure they are colouring the correct side of the paper. Paint a coloured wash over the top.

Once the wrapping paper is dry, staple the drawing of the toy on to the grey backing paper. Place the corresponding wrapping paper over it but only staple the top edge so that the wrapping paper forms a flap which can be lifted. If this assignment is set near Christmas, the pictures could be mounted on to a large sack or Christmas tree shape.

Discussion

As they draw, talk about the distinctive shape of the toy. How can they tell it's an aeroplane rather than a ball? Encourage them to include important shape details which give essential clues to each toy's identity.

If they need inspiration for the patterns on the wrapping paper, refer them back to the paper used to wrap the toys or suggest handwriting patterns. Remind them to press hard with the wax crayons so that the pattern will show through the wash. Encourage them to describe what happens when they apply the wash. Are there some colours which they cannot see very clearly?

Evaluation

Use the display to play a guessing game. point to each present in turn and ask a pupil to identify which toy is concealed under the wrapping paper. Once they have guessed, invite them to lift the flap to find out if they were correct. What clues in the shape helped them to guess? Which shape is the easiest to guess and why? Is there a shape which is very difficult to identify?

Follow-up

Make worksheets where the children need to use double-headed arrows to join a black silhouette shape to the corresponding picture. (Mathematics)

43

Butterflies

Objective
To learn the difference between plane shapes with curved and straight edges.

What you need
Small cards showing plane shapes illustrating curved and straight edges, butterfly specimens, photographs of butterflies, magnifying glasses, dark coloured sugar paper in two sizes, pencils, scissors, large gummed paper shapes (some with curved and some with straight edges), two different coloured plastic plates, PVA adhesive, glue sticks.

Preparation
Use the small cards to introduce the notion of shapes with curved or straight edges. Play sorting or matching games with the cards to reinforce the idea. Show the children the gummed paper shapes and invite them to sort them into sets with curved or straight edges.

If appropriate, take the children outside to look for butterflies. If not, use the photographs or specimens to stimulate a discussion about butterflies. Draw their attention to each butterfly's shape, size, colour, texture and various body parts. Look particularly at the shapes in the wing markings. Are there any shapes with curved edges? Which ones have shapes with straight edges? Magnifying glasses may well be a useful aid to children studying specimens.

What to do
Allow the children to choose the colour and size of their paper. Ask them to use the pencil to draw the main shapes of a butterfly. Refer them to the specimens or photographs for ideas on the overall shape of butterflies. Suggest they cut out their butterfly shape.

Explain that they are going to add wing markings to their butterfly using the gummed shapes. They will need to decide whether they are going to use shapes with straight edges or shapes with curved edges and stick them on to the wings of their butterfly. Although these shapes are supposed to have adhesive already on them, sometimes PVA is still needed to stick them successfully to sugar paper. More able children could also be encouraged to cut out their own shapes with curved or straight edges.

Discussion
Talk about the overall shape of their butterfly. How many wings will it have? Will they have rounded or jagged edges? Can they draw antennae? What colour is it? How many straight edges does it have? Does it remind them of something? Very young children will stick the shapes randomly all over the butterfly but more mature children could be encouraged to organise their picture. Can they make some of the shapes touch? Is it possible to copy an arrangement of spots on one of the specimens?

Evaluation

Discuss the finished butterflies. Can they point to a butterfly where all the shapes have curved edges? Look at a butterfly with straight edged shapes and count the number of shapes with four straight edges. Have any of the shapes been deliberately organised to create a particular pattern? Do any of the shapes remind them of something else?

Follow up

During a PE lesson, invite the children to use their bodies to make curved and straight shapes. (PE)

Wrapping paper

Objective

To understand that plane shapes can be repeated to form a pattern.

What you need

Wooden or plastic mosaics, examples of wrapping paper showing repeat patterns (preferably using plane shapes), a selection of objects (cardboard tubes, corks, bricks, plastic cubes, balsa wood, small plastic lids), three printing trays, printing ink (red, blue, yellow), dark coloured tissue paper in two sizes, a range of small boxes, card cut as gift tags, a hole punch, coloured wool, sticky tape.

Preparation

Use the wooden or plastic mosaics to remind the children of the names for each plane shape and to introduce the idea of repeating shape patterns. Make one or two patterns and ask the children to continue them. Then challenge them to design repeating patterns of their own. Can a friend continue their pattern? Show the children the wrapping paper and ask them to identify the repeating patterns. Talk about how the shapes and colours are repeated. What would they use the wrapping paper for? How would they fix it round a present?

What to do

Explain that they are going to print their own wrapping paper using the various objects. If they are unfamiliar with printing, allow them a period of free play with the objects on scrap paper. Allow them to choose the colour and size of their tissue paper then divide the objects amongst the three primary colours and stress the need to use each object with its allocated colour only.

On a spare piece of tissue, show them how to print a repeating pattern in a line across the paper working from left to right. Invite them to create their own repeating patterns in lines to cover the whole of the tissue, making a different pattern for each line. Allow the printing ink to dry then ask the children to use their wrapping paper to cover a small box and stick it down with tape. Suggest they make their own gift tag, punch a hole in it and fix it to the box with a short length of wool and some sticky tape.

Discussion

While they are printing, talk about the shapes the objects produce. Can they predict what shape their object will produce? Ask them to explain their repeating pattern. Are they repeating colours as well as shapes? Discuss any difficulties with the printing process and how to overcome these. For example, what happens to the print if the object is moved while pressing downwards? Why is it better to work from left to right and from top to bottom?

When they are wrapping their boxes, encourage them to find a way which will use the minimum amount of wrapping paper. Very young children tend to start by placing the object in the middle and gathering the paper round it. If appropriate, show them how to start by placing the box at the edge of the paper.

Evaluation

Talk about the wrapping paper the children have produced. Can they find examples of repeating patterns for both shape and colour? Choose one or two examples and ask them to match the object to the shapes on the wrapping paper. Are any of the prints smudged or unclear? Can they explain why this has happened and how to avoid it in future? Which wrapping paper do they like best and why? Look at the wrapped parcels. Which ones are wrapped neatly? Are there any alternatives to sticky tape which they could have used to secure the parcels?

Follow-up

Encourage the children to look for repeating shape patterns in the environment. Make a display of pictures and objects to support their findings. For example, they may find repeating shape patterns in bunting, wallpaper, clothing, curtains, carpets and buildings. (Art)

Musical instruments

Objective

To explore how new two-dimensional shapes can be created by overlapping other shapes.

What you need

Percussion instruments (tambourine, triangle, maracas, sleigh bells, two tone wood blocks, beaters), pale coloured sugar paper in two sizes, oil pastels, coloured Cellophane.

Preparation

Show the children the percussion instruments. If they are unfamiliar with them, allow them a period of free play. How do you play each one? What material is it made out of? Can they describe the sound it makes? Focus their attention on to the shape of each instrument. What shapes would they draw to represent each instrument?

Arrange three of the instruments on a table so that they overlap. Talk with the children about the meaning of this word. Explore several different arrangements and talk about the shapes each creates.

What to do

Allow each child to choose the colour and size of their paper. Ask them to choose one percussion instrument and draw a large picture of it using a light coloured oil pastel. Stress that they need only draw the main shapes and marks they can see.

Then suggest they choose a different instrument and draw a picture of it so that some part of it overlaps the previous drawing. Repeat this procedure with a third instrument, emphasising the need for part of the drawing to overlap one or both of the previous drawings. Invite the children to use the oil pastels to colour their drawing, choosing any colours they wish. Use a different colour for each new shape created by overlapping (see Figure 1). More mature children may wish to mix the oil pastel colours by placing one on top of another.

Discussion
As they draw, talk with them about the shapes they can see on each instrument. Refer them back to their chosen instrument to improve the quality of their drawing. Some children may be hesitant about drawing on top of a drawing so encourage them to be bold about overlapping their pictures. As they colour, draw their attention to the different plane shapes in their pictures, and particularly to the new shapes created where their drawings overlap.

Colour each area differently.

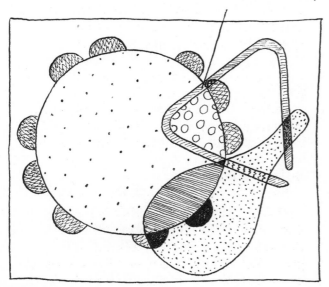

Figure 1

Evaluation
Choose two or three examples of the finished pictures and ask the children to name the percussion instruments featured in them. Talk about the shapes in each picture and especially those created by overlapping. Draw their attention to the shapes in the overall composition. Which pictures have the most interesting arrangements and why?

Follow-up
Give the children pieces of coloured Cellophane which have been cut into familiar plane shapes. Allow them to experiment with these pieces, encouraging them to overlap them to create new shapes. Can they place one piece on top of another to create an oblong, square or triangle where they overlap? (Art)

Fruit

Objective
To explore how a shape can be divided and rearranged to create a totally new shape.

What you need
A collection of fruit (with a variety of shapes), white A4 paper, soft pencils (6B), access to a photocopier, wax crayons, scissors, adhesive such as a Pritt stick.

Preparation
Show the children the collection of fruit. Allow them to handle them and encourage them to use their senses to explore each one. What does it smell like? Is the texture rough, smooth, hard or soft? How many colours can they see? Draw their attention to the overall shape of the fruit and compare it with the other fruits.

What to do

Explain to the children that they are going to produce a picture of one of the fruits and also invent a completely new one. Give each child an A4 piece of white paper and allow them to choose one of the fruits. Ask them to use their pencil to draw the most important lines to show the overall shape of their fruit. Encourage them to add any major spots, lines or blobs.

Photocopy each drawing and return the two identical pictures to the children. Ask them to use the wax crayons to colour both drawings in exactly the same way. Refer them back to the original fruit and encourage them to use realistic colours if possible.

Ask them to cut out their photocopied fruit, cut it into four or five pieces and then rearrange these pieces on another piece of A4 paper to create a totally new fruit with a completely different shape to the original. When they are happy with their arrangement, suggest they use the adhesive to stick the pieces down. Display the original drawing and the new 'invented' fruit alongside the real fruit which inspired the activity.

Discussion

As they draw, refer the children back to the real fruit and focus their attention on its shape. Is it completely round or does it have any bumps on it? What distinctive markings does it have? Is there a stalk or a leaf still attached? When they are colouring the two pictures of their fruit, encourage them to try to make them identical. Can they mix colours on their fruit by overlapping different coloured wax crayons? When they have cut out their photocopied fruit, stress the need to experiment with different arrangements before sticking the pieces down. Make sure all the pieces are used and none are lost.

Evaluation

Choose two or three different examples from the final display and discuss the shape of the original fruit and the original drawing. How well has the child managed to capture the shape and colour of the original fruit? Then compare the first drawing with the new 'invented' fruit. How has the overall shape of the fruit changed? Which shape is more interesting? Emphasise the link between the original drawing and the new 'invented' fruit. Do the children realise that they have simply reorganised the same shape by dividing it up?

Follow-up

Give the new 'invented' fruits a name by rearranging the letters of the original fruit. Write out the name of the original fruit, allow the children to cut it into individual letters and experiment with different arrangements of the letters. Help them pronounce their new 'invented' names and when they are satisfied with their arrangement, allow them to stick them on to a piece of paper and add it to the picture of their 'invented' fruit. (English)

Changing views

Objective
To find out how the shapes seen on objects change according to viewpoint.

What you need
White cartridge paper, pens, three familiar objects from the classroom which have very different front and top views, such as a xylophone, a toy cooker and a toy ironing board.

Preparation
Take each object in turn and discuss it with the children. Whereabouts is it kept in the classroom? What materials is it made from? How is it used? Draw their attention to the shapes they can see if they view it solely from the front. It may help to lift the objects on to a table so they are nearer to the children's eye level and they are then less distracted by the top view. Talk about what they can and cannot see from this viewpoint. Now place the objects on the floor and ask the children to stand over each object to study the top view. Discuss the shapes which the children can see now. Are they the same as those on the front view?

What to do
Give each child a piece of white cartridge paper and ask them to fold it in half. Allow them to choose which object they wish to draw. Ask them to draw the shapes they can see on the top of the object in the top half of the paper. Then invite them to draw the shapes they can see on the front view of the object in the bottom half of the paper. More mature children may be capable of drawing the back and side view of their object on another piece of paper. Display the objects and the final drawings together.

Discussion
As the children draw, encourage them to look carefully at the object and talk about the shapes they can see. How many circles can they see on the top of the toy cooker? Are they all the same size? How are they positioned? Can they count the number of oblongs on the top of the xylophone? What do they notice about the size of these oblongs? Encourage them to include the shape of screws or hinges in their drawings.

Evaluation
Look at the final display and discuss the different shapes in both the front and top view of each object. Which view is the most distinctive and therefore the easiest to recognise? Is there a view which is very difficult to recognise because the shapes could belong to several different objects?

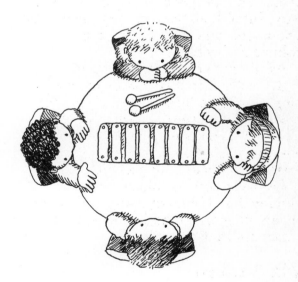

Follow-up
Link the above activity with geographical map-making skills. If the children have played with a train set or village playmat, suggest they draw maps of one of their layouts by recording all the shapes which they can see from above. (Geography)

Leaves

Objective
To introduce the idea of positive shapes (the shape of the objects) and negative shapes (the space in between the objects) (see the diagram on page 37).

What you need
A collection of house-plants with very differently shaped leaves, a collection of plane shapes (mosaics, Logic shapes), white card cut into small oblongs, pencils (6B), scissors, white cartridge paper, wax crayons.

Preparation
Show the children the house-plants and talk about them in general. Name the various parts of the plants. What are the similarities and differences between them? Focus their attention on the leaves of each one. What colour are they? Do they have markings? Are they hairy? What shape are they? What pattern do the veins make?

Use the plane shapes to introduce the idea of positive and negative shapes. Make an arrangement of shapes leaving spaces in between. Ask the children to describe the spaces in between.

Allow them a period of free play to design and discuss their own arrangements.

What to do
Explain to the children that they are going to make their own template of a leaf.

Give them a small piece of card and a pencil. Ask them to choose one of the house-plants and draw the shape of one leaf from observation. Encourage them to fill their piece of card with their drawing and avoid any details. They can then cut out their leaf with some help from an adult if the card is difficult to cut.

Give them a piece of white cartridge paper and ask them to draw round their leaf template. Invite them to move their template to a different position and draw round it again. Repeat this process but try to make interesting shapes in between the leaves. Encourage them to fill the majority of the space on their paper.

Refer them back to their original house-plant leaf and ask them to draw the veins on each of their leaves. Then suggest they choose one wax crayon and colour the spaces in between their leaves. Display the original leaf and the templates alongside the final pictures.

Discussion
As the children draw their leaf, talk with them about the distinctive features of its shape. Does it have a smooth or jagged edge? Is there a long or short stem? Is the leaf made up of several smaller shapes? Discuss the shapes which are beginning to appear in between their drawings of leaves. Does it help to make some of the drawings touch each other? Encourage them to look carefully before drawing the veins on their leaves. Are the lines straight or curved? How are they structured? When the children are colouring in the negative shapes, ask them to describe the shapes.

Evaluation

Discuss the display and focus on the negative shapes. Which picture do the children think has the most interesting shapes in between the leaves? Why? Choose one or two examples and ask a child to describe the shapes seen. Compare the overall shapes of the leaf templates. Which are similar and why?

Follow-up

Go for a walk round the school and look for the negative shapes in between objects. For example, the shapes in between railings or fencing, large PE apparatus or chairs. (Art)

Rocks and pebbles

Objective

To use photographs of sculpture by Barbara Hepworth to inspire clay sculptures based on rocks and pebbles.

What you need

Two or three photographs of sculpture with holes in by Barbara Hepworth (*The Complete Sculpture of Barbara Hepworth 1960–69* by Alan Bowness, Lund Humphries), a collection of rocks and pebbles with holes in, clay, modelling tools including wire-ended tools.

Preparation

Show the children two or three examples of sculpture with holes in by Barbara Hepworth and discuss them. What are the similarities/differences? What materials do they think each is made from? What is the difference between a sculpture and a painting? Discuss the fact that the photographs only show us one view of the sculpture. What do the sculptures make the children think of? Explain that Barbara Hepworth was often inspired by rocks and pebbles. Show them the collection of rocks and pebbles and discuss two or three of them in detail. What shape is the rock? Can you see through the holes? Encourage the children to describe the shape of the holes.

What to do

Invite the children to choose a rock or pebble as a basis for their work. Give them a small lump of clay and ask them to make it into a sphere, using their hands to pat or roll it into shape and to smooth any cracks. Ask them to look carefully at the shape of their rock or pebble and to try to make their ball of clay into a similar shape by pushing and squeezing it. Refer them back to their rock or pebble for the size, shape and position of the holes. Show them how to use a wire-ended modelling tool to make a hole in clay.

Children who have been introduced to texture can refer back to their rock or pebble to look for any textures on the surface. Encourage them to use the modelling tools to create textures on their clay shapes. Let them experiment on a spare piece of clay if they are not sure how to create a texture.

Leave the clay shapes to dry. As the clay will dry to a brown or grey 'rock' colour, you may prefer to display them as they are. If you intend to fire them in a kiln, make sure they are not too thick.

Hollow out any which may be too thick from the base. Display the finished sculptures with the rocks and pebbles and the photographs of Barbara Hepworth's sculptures.

Discussion
When the children are looking at their chosen rock or pebble, encourage them to describe what they see in detail. It is not intended that the children should try to make an exact replica of their rock but rather that their own firsthand observations should focus their attention and enrich their work. Are their holes going to pierce the whole clay shape or are they only going half way through? How many holes will there be and will they all be the same size and shape? If they are going to apply a texture, will it cover the whole of their sculpture or only part of it? Remind them to turn their clay shape round and view it from different angles. Display the Barbara Hepworth photographs nearby so you can refer to the shapes and holes on her sculptures.

Evaluation
Discuss the final display and compare the children's work with Barbara Hepworth's sculptures. Do any have a similar overall shape or the same number and shape of holes? Can they match the real rock or pebble to the sculpture which was based on it? Which sculpture would they most like to touch and why?

Follow-up
Encourage the children to make a collection of objects with holes in them. Which holes are regular or irregular shapes? Try looking through them at a picture and discussing how much can be seen. (Science)

Trees

Objective
To link Gustav Klimt's 'Tree of Life' frieze to the children's experience of shape and pattern.

What you need
A copy of the 'Tree of Life' frieze by Gustav Klimt (*Gustav Klimt* by G. Fliedl, Taschen), pale beige or cream coloured sugar paper, paints (red, yellow and blue), thick and thin brushes, water pots, palettes, printing inks (black, white, yellow, red and blue), printing trays, objects for printing such as cardboard tubes, corks, Multilink cubes, Unifix cubes, old Plasticine (which the children can mould into shapes and use as a stamp), balsa wood.

Preparation

Show the children Klimt's 'Tree of Life' frieze and discuss the overall shape of the tree. Does it look like a real tree? What is unusual about it? What shapes and patterns can they see? How are they organised? Are they all over the tree or on selected areas? Do any of the shapes join to make a repeating pattern? Encourage them to look for shapes within shapes.

Take the children outside and look carefully at a real tree. It is helpful if the children can look at trees without leaves in the winter months. Name the various parts of the tree and discuss its overall structure. Which is the thickest part of the tree? Are the branches curved or straight? Is the tree tall and thin or short and wide?

What to do

Display the 'Tree of Life' by Klimt nearby for reference. Give the children a large piece of sugar paper and ask them to mix their own 'brown' colour using the red, yellow and blue paint. When they have produced a colour which they like, ask them to use it to paint a large tree on to their paper. Invite them to choose different sized brushes when appropriate. Allow the paint to dry.

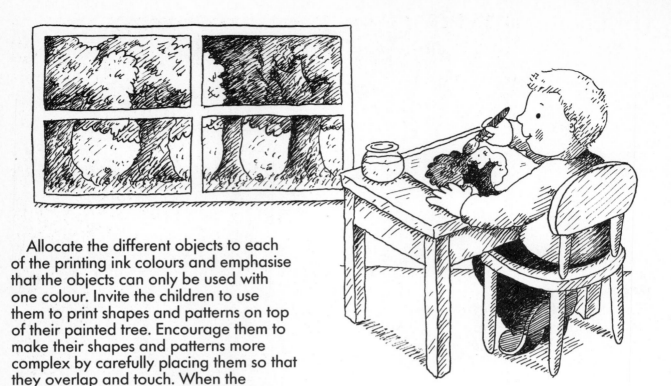

Allocate the different objects to each of the printing ink colours and emphasise that the objects can only be used with one colour. Invite the children to use them to print shapes and patterns on top of their painted tree. Encourage them to make their shapes and patterns more complex by carefully placing them so that they overlap and touch. When the pictures are dry, display them alongside the Klimt frieze.

Discussion

Talk with the children as they mix their brown colour. Can they describe the colour? Did they use more yellow or more red? How could they make it darker or lighter? When they begin to paint their tree, remind them of the shapes used by Klimt and their own firsthand observations of trees outside. Will their tree have straight, curved or even spiralling branches? Which brush would they use to make thin branches or twigs?

If they have not used the objects for printing before, give them some scrap paper to experiment. Refer them back to Klimt's picture before they print. can they print shapes within shapes or make similar patterns? Encourage them to be selective about where they place their shapes and patterns. Can they group them together rather than printing them randomly?

Evaluation

Discuss the pictures, focusing on the shapes used and the way in which they have been organised. Choose one or two examples and ask the children to say which are the most interesting parts of the tree and why. Have any of the children included features directly inspired by Klimt such as spiralling branches or shapes within shapes?

Follow-up

Klimt's original 'Tree of Life' frieze was commissioned for the walls of the dining room in the Stoclet Palace, Brussels. Invite the children to compile a list of places in their own local environment where they have seen wall friezes, for example, on the outside of buildings, inside shops or shopping precincts, churches or local historic houses. If possible, make a photographic record of some of these to use as a basis for discussion. (Art)

Colour

Chapter three

Colours can be fascinating to young children but it is unwise to assume that because they are surrounded by colour, they will necessarily have thought about them. Early years teachers can devise activities to introduce children to the exciting world of colour and develop their understanding.

Teaching strategies

Initially children need to learn the colour names, including the less obvious ones such as grey, brown and pink. This can be achieved through a whole multitude of cross-curricular activities as well as art-based assignments. Wearing dressing-up clothes of one colour, building with bricks of a single colour or grouping farm animals in separate fields according to colour are all incidental ways in which colour names can be learned. More structured activities could include colour-based games, sorting toys into sets of colours or matching pictures according to colour.

Any art activity which involves the use of coloured materials can also support the learning of colour names. Remember to provide a broad range of coloured media (play dough, pastels, felt-tipped pens, fabrics) and not just to limit the children to paint. Initially, ready-mixed paint in non-spill pots is advisable and for some children, learning to put the paintbrush into the correct pot is quite difficult.

Many early years pupils often use colour in a symbolic way in that they will tend to choose a colour for emotional reasons, not because it is an accurate representation of whatever they are drawing or painting. Blue faces and red snowmen would not be uncommon in their work. It is important to allow young children to use colour in this way and not to damage their self-confidence by inappropriate remarks.

If the children have become confident in using paints mixed by an adult, introduce them to the idea of mixing their own coloured paints either on the paper itself or in a special mixing palette. Colour mixing can prove to be a magical experience and many children enjoy stirring different colours together so much that they forget to apply it to the paper! First of all, encourage free play with the colours, but eventually it is appropriate to structure the play by limiting the choice of colours and setting a particular task. At first, the subject for any colour-mixing activity should be fairly straightforward so that they are painting within a large, simple shape (a kite or umbrella) and do not have to worry about a subject with intricate details. Initially, they will tend to paint random patches all over the shape but as they mature, they will begin to organise the paint within the shape.

Although paint is the most flexible way of exploring colour, it is not the only vehicle, for chalks, oil pastels, wax crayons, coloured pencils, felt-tipped pens, coloured Cellophane and Plasticine can all make an important contribution to understanding colour mixing.

Through carefully designed activities, they will begin to realise that primary colours (red, blue, yellow — a primary colour is one which cannot be made by mixing other colours together) can be mixed to produce secondary colours (orange, green, violet). It will be necessary to repeat these activities within a wide range of contexts before children remember the constancy of such phenomena, that is, that red and yellow mix together to produce a variation of orange. Initially, children should be allowed to experiment freely with colour-mixing. When they are confident with this process, they can be asked to try to match their colours to real objects.

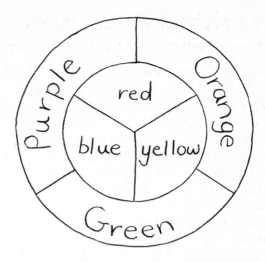

Once they have mastered the colour names, they can be introduced to the idea of colour families, so they begin to appreciate that there is more than one kind of red as well as many different tones. Sorting activities which involve grouping coloured objects or pictures into 'families' will help them begin to identify similarities and differences between tones.

Simple aspects of tone can be introduced by setting tasks which develop the children's ability to identify light and dark colours. It is also worth devising the occasional activity which examines the effect of adding white or black paint to the primary colours. Some young children are very fond of black paint and use it indiscriminately, often producing dull, sombre paintings. By deliberately focusing on the effects of black paint, children will learn to use it cautiously and to select it for appropriate subject matter. For the majority of colour-mixing activities, it is better not to offer children black paint but to encourage them to find other ways of making colours darker. Many adult artists (especially Impressionist painters) often avoid using black because of its gloomy effect. Children can also be introduced to the idea that tone can be altered by the consistency of the paint — the more water added, the lighter the colour. This is a basic concept for future work with watercolours.

More difficult ideas about colour can be introduced through many everyday early years activities. Threading beads in regular colour sequences can lead into work involving colour patterns while discussions about road safety usually touch on bright and dull colours. Looking through coloured Cellophanes or tissue paper can introduce the idea that colour can be transparent, translucent or opaque.

Children who have been introduced to the various aspects of colour outlined above, can begin to investigate more abstract notions. Even quite young children associate red, yellow and orange (hot colours) with hot things such as the sun or fire. On the other hand, white, blue and grey (cold colours) are frequently linked with cold things such as snowmen, rainy weather or the sea. Similarly, many children readily discuss 'happy' or 'sad' colours. Although young children do not consciously manipulate these qualities of colour in their own work as an adult artist would, they are often surprisingly sophisticated in interpreting them in the work of others.

Children's development in art is not a clear-cut linear process but frequently moves backwards and forwards between stages. Many young children may be quite capable of understanding simple colour mixing and using it appropriately in a structured activity but may still choose to use colour symbolically when given a free choice. To deny them access to colour-mixing activities is to limit drastically their experiences of colour and to prevent many from extending their understanding of it.

At the end of the chapter two activities link the children's own experiences of colour with mature artists – Claude Monet and Edvard Munch. Before offering these activities, it is important for the children to have experienced some of the previous activities. For the Monet activity, children need a great deal of colour-mixing experience and must be able to identify light and dark colours; for the Munch activity, they need an understanding of 'hot' colours and the use of colour to convey emotion.

Bubbles

Objective
To examine the effect of mixing red and blue paint.

What you need
Bubble mixture, pale grey sugar paper, straws, red and blue paint, small plastic tubs (cottage cheese/margarine containers), water, scissors, three circular objects to draw round (large, medium, small), plastic droppers.

Preparation
Blow bubbles for the children to observe. Discuss their size, shape, colour and how they move. Encourage them to notice what happens to the liquid on the bubble as it moves and how this affects the colours produced. What is inside the bubble? Watch carefully to see what happens when a bubble pops. Allow the children to play with the plastic droppers in the water tray so that they are familiar with their use.

What to do
Explain to the children that they are going to make pictures of bubbles using a straw blowing technique. Firstly, ask them to draw round several of the circular objects on a piece of grey sugar paper so they will have different sized bubble shapes and cut them out.

Invite the children to help add water to the red and blue paint to make a watery consistency in the tubs. Suggest they choose one colour and use a plastic dropper to place a blob of paint on to their grey bubble before blowing carefully with the straw to create an interesting shape. If necessary, encourage them to add more paint so the blown shapes cover the majority of the 'bubble'. Repeat the process with a second colour, blowing with the straw to mix the two colours in some areas. The bubbles are most effective when the two primary colours can still be seen in their pure form in some places as well as having some areas where the colours have mixed. Very young children often need prompting as to when to stop blowing! Repeat the process on the other bubble shapes.

When the paint is dry, staple the bubbles on and around a poem about bubbles. Although the poem could be chosen from a published anthology, it is more relevant if the poem has been written by the children as a collaborative activity based on their firsthand observations.

Discussion
Encourage the children to experiment with the straw (but remind them not to suck!). What happens if they blow softly/very hard? Does it make any difference if they blow straight down on top of the paint or with the straw at an angle? Can they predict what will happen when the two colours merge? Are there variations in the secondary colour (purple) depending upon the proportions of the two primary colours? Why does the paint need to be watery?

Evaluation
Compare and discuss the results of colour mixing. Does red and blue always produce a variation of purple? Which bubble has more blue paint on it? What effect does this have on the red? Can the children point to a purple where more red has been used?

Follow up
Mix red and blue using a different media, such as chalks, pastels or oil crayons. Encourage the children to overlap the same two primary colours to see whether the same secondary colour results. (Art)

Suns

Objective
To examine the effect of mixing red and yellow paint.

What you need
White cartridge paper cut into two sizes, red and yellow paints, water pots, printing trays or plates, a collection of small pieces of sponge with different textures, brushes, scissors, small pieces of white cartridge paper for hats, red and yellow oil pastels, a stapler.

Preparation
Learn the song 'The Sun Has Got His Hat On'. Ask the children what colours they think the sun would be? What expression do they think the sun would be wearing?

What to do
Explain to the children that they are going to make a large picture of a sun with a face. They will make the hat separately and add it later and so do not need to worry about including it in their initial picture. Allow them to choose the size of their paper and stress the need for the sun picture to fill the paper.

Invite them to dab the pure yellow paint with a sponge on to their picture. Wash the sponge in the water pot and then dab on pure red paint. Suggest they try using the brushes to mix different proportions of red and yellow paint and

apply the resulting colours to their picture with a sponge. Remind them to wash the sponge and the brush before using a new colour. Once the children have sponge printed a sun shape with no white spaces, suggest they add features (eyes, nose, mouth, rays) with a brush. When the paintings are dry, cut them out.

Give them the small pieces of white cartridge paper and ask them to use the red and yellow oil pastels to draw and colour a hat for their sun. Suggest they mix the colours by overlapping them and blending them with their fingers. Cut out the finished hat and staple it to the sun face.

Discussion
Before the children start mixing the red and yellow paint, ask them to predict the resulting colour. Can they describe the colours they have made as they mix them? Did they use more yellow or more red? Does the colour they have made remind them of something? Encourage them to overlap colours as they sponge print. Can they describe any new colours they make? Compare the marks made by the sponges with those made by the brushes. How are they different? Talk about the colours the children mix with the oil pastels. Do the oil pastels mix to produce a shade of orange?

Evaluation

Talk about the colours in the final sun pictures. Find where the red and yellow have been used in their pure form and where they have been mixed. How did the children make a pale orange? Can they describe how to make a darker orange? Which sun do they like best and why?

Follow-up

Suggest the children write poems entitled 'Red is . . .', 'Yellow is . . .', or 'Orange is . . .'. For example, 'Red is . . . a rosy apple, as hot as fire, bright like poppies and dangerous to touch.' (English)

Dragons

Objective

To examine the effect of mixing yellow and blue paint.

What you need

A collection of pictures of dragons (illustrations from stories or poems, try to include multicultural examples, such as Chinese), white cartridge paper in two sizes, yellow and blue paints, water pots, palettes, thick and thin brushes.

Preparation

Show the children the collection of pictures of dragons. Talk about their overall body shape and then focus on the shape of particular features such as their tail, head and wings. Look for similarities and differences in the pictures. What colour are the dragons?

What to do

Explain to the children that they are going to paint a picture of a dragon. Allow them to choose the size and position of their paper (landscape or portrait). Show them how to make a yellow wash by adding water to yellow paint and then cover one side of the paper with the wash. Then suggest they use a light blue wash to map out the main shapes of their dragon. Invite the children to use the pure yellow and pure blue to

paint some parts of their dragon then suggest they experiment by mixing different proportions of blue and yellow paint and use the resulting colours to paint other areas. Remind them to wash the brush in between mixing colours and refer them back to the collection of pictures for ideas on details such as claws, scales and spikes. Display the children's paintings alongside the original dragon pictures.

Discussion

Before they start mixing, ask the children to predict what colour blue and yellow will make. Talk with them about their colours. Can they describe how they made a colour? Did they use more yellow or more blue? Can they describe the resulting green? Which are light and which are dark?

Evaluation

Talk with the children about the final display. Can they point to examples of pure yellow and pure blue on the dragon paintings? What did adding water to make a wash do to these colours? Discuss the various greens which have been produced by mixing yellow and blue. Which dragons have a wide range of greens? Do any of the greens remind the children of something?

Follow-up

Cut up two identical commercial paint charts which show various shades of green. Challenge the children to match the colours exactly. (Mathematics)

Autumn leaves

Objective

To mix colours to match those found in brown leaves.

What you need

A collection of autumn leaves, commercial paint colour charts, white cartridge paper, brushes, palettes, water pots, a limited range of paints, for example red, yellow, blue, orange, white, soft black pencils (6B), scissors, magnifying glasses.

Preparation

Encourage the children to look carefully at the collection of autumn leaves with the magnifying glasses. Focus upon the colour of the leaves. How many different colours can they identify? Are all the brown colours exactly the same? Does a particular brown remind them of something else, perhaps in the classroom? Sort the brown leaves into sets of similar shades of brown.

Show the children some commercial paint colour charts for brown and discuss the names. Can they match any of the leaves to a particular brown on the chart?

What to do

Ask each child to choose one autumn leaf which they would like to paint. Give each a large piece of white paper and suggest they mix a pale brown to paint the basic shape of a giant leaf. Encourage them to paint the whole of their leaf leaving no white spaces. Advise them to ignore the background because the leaf will be cut out when finished. Experiment with mixing brown colours to match those on their real leaf.

Once the paintings are dry, cut out the leaves. Refer the children back to their real leaf and ask them to observe the lines formed by the veins. Can they use a pencil to draw similar lines on top of the paint on their leaf? If there are any dark spots or patches on their real leaf, encourage them to try to draw these also. Display the painted leaves alongside the real leaves.

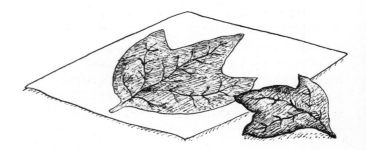

Discussion

While the children are mixing the various brown colours, talk about how difficult or easy it is to match exactly the colours on the real leaves. What colour could they add to match it more closely? Can they predict what effect it will have? Does their brown remind them of something else? Can they invent a name for their colour?

Discuss the appearance of the veins on the real leaves before and while the children are drawing them on to their painted leaves. Are they straight or curved? Are they thick or thin lines? Do they cover the whole or only part of the leaf? Remind the children to press hard with their pencil to make their lines show up on top of the paint. What happens if they press lightly?

Evaluation

Discuss the final display with the children. Which leaves do they think are most successful and why? Look closely at one or two and count how many different shades of brown have been used. Identify the lightest or darkest brown.

Follow-up

Ask the children to think of one sense at a time in relation to the real leaves and to brainstorm a list of descriptive words, for example, sound — crunchy, crackly, rustling, whispering. Suggest they choose the most interesting words and write them individually as labels to add to the display of painted and real leaves. (English)

Yarn wrapping

Objective

To distinguish between light and dark colours.

What you need

Strong card in the three primary colours (cut into oblongs), double-sided tape, a variety of yarns in the three primary colours including a wide range of shades from light to dark, scissors.

Preparation

Show the children the collection of yarns and invite them to sort the yarns into colour families. Look at each family in turn, encouraging the children to identify the light and dark colours.

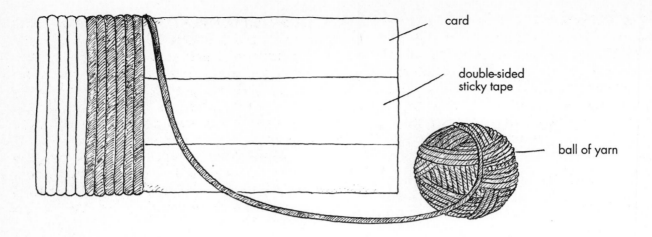

card

double-sided
sticky tape

ball of yarn

What to do

Stick a strip of double-sided tape down the middle of each piece of card (widthways) on both the front and back then allow the children to choose the colour of their piece of card. Explain that they are going to wrap the yarns around the card (lengthways). The yarns must belong to the same colour family as the colour of their card. More mature children can be encouraged to create a sequence of light and dark colours. Show the children how to start at the back of the card and wrap the yarn round it several times, pressing it firmly on to the tape both back and front to form a band of colour. Cut the yarn so that it finishes at the back. Invite the children to repeat this process with different coloured yarns until their card is covered with bands of colour. Younger children will tend to place the colours randomly while more mature children can be encouraged to work from one side to the other to create a sequence.

Discussion

As the children work, talk with them about the colours they are choosing. Does it belong to the same colour family as their card? Is it a light or dark colour? Do they have any clothing that colour?

Evaluation

Compare and contrast the finished cards. Which ones belong to the same colour family? Choose two or three examples of the same colour family and identify the light and dark colours. Which card has the darkest or lightest colour? Can the children identify any sequences?

Follow-up

Invite the children to help make a collection of clothing belonging to one colour family. Discuss the different shades of colour and try putting three or four of the items of clothing in order from light to dark. (Art and Mathematics)

Candles

Objective

To examine the effect of adding white to primary colours.

What you need

A collection of candles (different shapes, colours, sizes), white cartridge paper, yellow chalk, a limited range of paints, such as red, blue, yellow (the primary colours) and white, thick and thin brushes, palettes, water pots, scissors, plastic droppers, black backing paper, a stapler.

Preparation

Allow the children to explore the collection of candles, focusing on their size, shape, colour and texture. Light one or two to allow children to observe them when alight. Consider safety precautions: ensure that candles are placed on non-flammable surfaces and warn children about the dangers of touching the flame.

Allow the children to use the droppers in the water tray to make sure they are familiar with their use before this assignment.

What to do

Use their observations of candles to inspire their own drawing of a candle which can then provide the basis for an investigation into colour mixing. Ask the children to use the yellow chalk to map out lightly the overall shape of a candle but with no fine details because the candle will be painted. Refer them back to the collection of candles to remind them of the various possibilities for the shape. Explain that no background is required as the candles will be cut out when finished.

Invite them to choose one of the primary colours and a thick brush. Explain that they are going to paint bands (horizontal or vertical) across their candle in various shades of their chosen primary colour. The bands can be narrow or wide but must eventually cover the whole candle leaving no white spaces. They can place the bands at any point on the candle and need not necessarily work from top to bottom.

Ask them to put some of their primary colour into a palette and use this in its pure form for their first band. Explain that they then need to use the droppers to add a tiny amount of white paint to change the colour slightly before painting the next band. This procedure is then repeated, adding a small amount of white each time until the whole candle is covered with bands of colour. Allow the paint to dry. Suggest the children choose a different primary colour and a thin brush to apply patterns along the bands. Again, use the pure colour for the first band and then add small amounts of white paint for each successive band of pattern.

When the paint is dry, cut the candles out. Mount them on black backing paper, bending them slightly before stapling to create a three-dimensional effect.

Discussion

Invite the children to predict what will happen to their colour when white is added. Once they start mixing, talk to them about how their colour changes. Can they see the subtle change in tone each time white is added?

Talk about the reasons for changing to a thin brush to apply the decoration. Suggest handwriting patterns if they are unsure of what patterns to use. Does their second primary colour behave in the same way when white is added? More mature children could be asked how they are going to choose which band to decorate. For example, would their pure second colour be most effective applied to a pale or dark first band? Through discussion, some children may begin to appreciate the idea of contrast using dark on light and vice versa.

Evaluation

Look at the display of candles and discuss the effect that white has on colours. Focus on one or two candles and ask children to point to the darkest/lightest colours. Have two children managed to mix the same shade of blue?

Follow-up

Use the display of candles to compare sizes and reinforce taller than and shorter than. (Mathematics)

Monsters

Objective

To examine the effect of adding black to primary colours.

What you need

White cartridge paper, black sugar paper, felt-tipped pens, different sized brushes, water pots, palettes, plastic droppers, red, blue, yellow (primary colours) and black paints.

Preparation

Read the children stories or poems about monsters which live in dark places and take the opportunity to discuss their fears about monsters and the dark. Poems — 'Under the Stairs' and 'Scary Things' in *A Very First Poetry Book* (OUP), 'The Bad Dream' in *Smile Please* (Young Puffin) and 'Bump' in *Rhyme Time* (Beaver Books); stories — *The Owl Who Was Afraid of the Dark* by J. Tomlinson (Young Puffin), *Where the Wild Things Are* by M. Sendak (Bodley Head), *The Ankle Grabber* by R. Impey (Ragged Bears Ltd) and *The Monster Bed* by S. Varley (Andersen Press).

Make a visual aid to inspire discussion about a monster with two big bright eyes (see Figure 1). With the black sugar paper covering the whole of the monster apart from its eyes, ask the children questions which will build up an image in their imaginations. What dark place does it live in? Why are its eyes so bright? Is it nice or nasty? What does it look like? How does it move? At the end of the discussion, ask a volunteer to lift up the black paper to reveal your monster. Draw a friendly monster with a smiley face to reassure those who may be worried by monsters. Don't spend too long looking at your drawing of a monster otherwise the children may only remember your image. Emphasise that they are going to paint their own personal monster and that each one should show whether it is a nice or nasty monster.

Allow the children to experiment with the droppers in the water tray before starting.

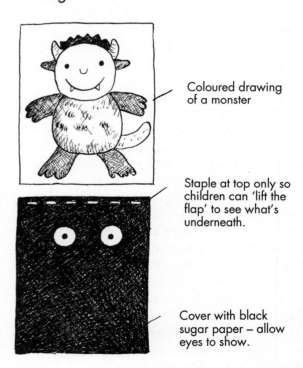

Coloured drawing of a monster

Staple at top only so children can 'lift the flap' to see what's underneath.

Cover with black sugar paper — allow eyes to show.

Figure 1

What to do

Ask the children to decide in which position to place their paper, landscape or portrait. Explain that if they want a monster with a long body, then landscape is the best position for the paper. Suggest they ignore the background as the painting will be cut out. Ask them to choose a primary colour to paint two large eyes. Allow them to use other primary colours if they wish to add pupils or outer rings to their eyes.

In a water pot, have some black paint thinned slightly with water so it can be picked up easily with a dropper. Remind the children how to use the dropper and suggest they use it to add small amounts of black to each primary colour. Each time they create a new colour, they should use it to paint part of their monster. Encourage them to use different sized brushes and to put textures or patterns on top of areas which they have already painted. Suggest the monster should eventually fill most of the paper. When the paintings are dry, cut the monsters out and display them together as a frieze.

Discussion

As the children work, ask questions to remind them of their imaginary monster. Does it have wings? How many legs has it got? Is it furry, feathery or wrinkled? Why is it important to add black only a few drops at a time? Can they describe what happens to a colour each time they add black? Do the children notice that some colours are totally changed? For example, yellow becomes green when black is added. When working on top of areas which they have already painted, discuss how well the second colour shows up and encourage them to consider this when deciding where to place a colour.

Evaluation

Discuss the display with the children. Which monsters look friendly? Is there a monster with eyes that would really make you jump if you found it under your bed? Choose one or two colours on the monsters and ask the children which colours they think were mixed to make them? Help the children to see that adding black has made the colours gloomy and dull. Explain that many artists want to avoid this and so rarely choose to use black either on its own or mixed with other colours. Can the children think of gloomy subjects where adding black to colours would be appropriate?

Follow-up

Suggest the children dictate or write a profile for their monster — what it looks like, how it moves, what it eats, its favourite activity and so on. They could then try matching the profiles to the different monsters. (English)

Water toys

Objective

To examine how adding water can alter the tone of a colour.

What you need

White cartridge paper, blue paint, brushes, palettes, water pots, plastic droppers, margarine tubs, washing-up liquid, straws, a collection of water toys (boats, waterwheels, plastic animals), scissors, PVA adhesive.

Preparation

Allow the children to play with the water toys in the water tray. Discuss in detail what each one looks like, how it works, what it is made from and so on. Make sure the children have had time to play with the droppers and know how to use them to manipulate liquid.

What to do

Ask each child to choose a water toy to paint and decide whether to have the paper in the landscape or portrait position. Show them how to mix a pale blue wash (add a tiny amount of blue paint to water) and suggest they use this to paint the overall shape of the water toy, only recording the most important shapes and lines. Stress the need to fill the paper with the picture.

Invite the children to use the pure blue paint to colour the darkest areas of their water toy. With the aid of the droppers, ask them to add a few drops of water to the blue paint and use the new colour to paint another part of their picture. Continue adding water and using the different tones of blue, working from the darkest to the lightest areas on their painting. Leave the pictures to dry.

Mix blue paint, washing-up liquid and water in the margarine tubs and use the straws to blow bubbles in this liquid. Once the bubbles have risen slightly above the rim, place a piece of white cartridge paper gently over the top to take a print. Repeat this procedure, overlapping the prints until the whole sheet of paper is covered in bubble prints. Encourage the children to experiment by gradually adding more blue paint to create darker prints. Once the bubble prints are dry, cut them into smaller pieces and stick them around the painting of the water toy. Display the finished pictures alongside the water toys which inspired them.

Discussion

Encourage the children to look carefully at their toy while painting. Can they describe what happens to the blue paint as they add increasing amounts of water? When making the bubble prints, remind them not to suck on the straws. What is inside the bubbles? How does the colour of the bubbles change as they add more blue paint? Would it work without the washing-up liquid? Encourage them to be selective about where they stick the bubble prints. Place the cut out pieces of bubble print on to the picture and experiment with different arrangements before sticking them down.

Evaluation

Choose one or two paintings and focus on the water toy. Can the children point to the darkest or lightest areas? Which shade would have most water or most paint? Ask one or two children to describe the bubble printing process. Identify dark and light areas on the bubble prints. Would any of the children change any aspect of their picture if they could do it again?

Follow-up

How does adding water alter the colour of other art materials? Try felt-tipped pens, coloured pencils, wax crayons, chalks and oil pastels. (Art and Science)

Fish

Objective
To repeat colours to create patterns.

What you need
Tropical fish (real or good photographs) or dead fish from the fishmongers, paper in a range of pale colours, white chalks, printing inks, printing trays, newspaper, sponges, a range of materials (corks, old Plasticine, bits of balsa wood or dowel, cotton buds, plastic bottle lids, cotton reels), scissors.

Preparation
Encourage the children to look carefully at the fish, noticing their shape, colours, size, body parts and methods of movement. Emphasise particularly any colour patterns (for example, red and black stripes) decorating the body.

What to do
Allow the children to choose the colour of their paper and ask them to use the chalk to map out the main shapes of a fish. Refer them back to the examples to gather ideas on body shape and remind them to draw the fish large enough to fill the paper. As the fish will be cut out when finished, ask them to ignore the background and avoid drawing fine details which will be hidden by the printing.

As many tropical fish are striped, show the children how newspaper can be used to mask and create a stripy pattern. Cut or tear strips of newspaper, dampen them slightly with a sponge and lay them over the fish shape (horizontally or vertically), leaving a gap between each one. Dip a sponge into a coloured ink (spread evenly on a printing tray) and dab the colour over the gaps left by the newspaper. Peel the newspaper off and coloured stripes should be revealed. Repeat the process with clean newspaper masking all or part of the previous colour and print with a second colour. This can be repeated as often as the children like.

Once the fish have a striped body, encourage the children to use the various materials dipped in ink to continue to decorate their fish with repeating patterns. Suggest they experiment by overlapping colours to create more complex patterns. Once the paintings are dry, cut them out and display them together as an underwater frieze.

Discussion
Focus the children's attention upon the colour patterns that they are making. For example, if they are using alternate red and green stripes, have they managed to produce a correct colour sequence? Similarly, when they are printing with the various materials remind them to consider the colour patterns.

The lollipop person

Evaluation
Discuss the finished frieze with the class. Ask the children to point out any colour patterns that they can see on any of the fish. Which patterns use two colours? Are there any which use three or more colours? Which fish do they think has the most interesting pattern and why? Can anyone describe the masking technique that they used to create stripes? Choose one or two fish and ask the children to show which materials they used to create their patterns, for example corks for circles, balsa for rectangles.

Follow-up
Make a collection of objects and/or fabrics with repeating colour patterns. Encourage the children to try to describe the patterns precisely without naming the object so that others can identify it. (Mathematics and Art)

Objective
To distinguish between dull and bright colours.

What you need
A visit by a lollipop person, white cartridge paper, wax crayons (including fluorescent ones if possible), sponges, black wash, coloured squares and black backing paper.

Preparation
Invite the lollipop person to talk to the children, focusing especially on the colours of her clothing and her lollipop sign. Discuss the safety reasons for using fluorescent and bright colours. Try darkening the room and shining a torch on to the clothing to discover any reflective areas. Place a variety of coloured squares against black backing paper and discuss which colours are brightest and therefore show up most easily.

What to do

Sort the wax crayons into bright and dull colours and discard the dull ones. Ask the children to draw and colour a large picture of the lollipop person on their piece of white paper using the wax crayons. Encourage them to include details such as her hat, belt, shoes and lollipop sign. Suggest they press hard and leave no white spaces. Apply the black wash with a sponge over the top of their pictures. The waxed areas should resist the paint, giving the impression of the lollipop person in the dark.

Discussion

When sorting the wax crayons, refer the children back to the lollipop person's clothing and the experiments with the coloured squres against a black background. As they draw, talk about the colours they choose. Which colour do they think is the brightest? Is one yellow brighter than another? Encourage the children to observe closely when they apply the black wash and to try to describe what happens.

Evaluation

Look carefully at the finished pictures and compare the results. Discuss how well the colours show up against the black wash. Which is the brightest/dullest colour? Were there any surprises? For example, did an apparently bright colour not show up as well as expected? Why was this?

Follow-up

Test out some of the dull wax crayons on a separate piece of paper, covering them with a black wash. Which appear brightest/dullest? Why would these colours not be suitable for a lollipop person? Look at the colours of the children's clothing and discuss how easy it would be to see them in the dark. Do any of them wear fluorescent arm bands, belts, badges or stickers? (Art and Science)

The sky

Objective

To introduce the idea that colour can be transparent, translucent or opaque depending upon the materials used.

What you need

Clear polythene bags cut into single sheets, PVA adhesive, scissors, masking tape, thin strips of dark blue card, sky-coloured collage materials — tissue paper, sugar paper, crêpe paper, Cellophane, coloured plastic bags.

Preparation

Take the children outside to look at the sky, preferably on a day when the sky has a wide variety of colours and interesting cloud formations. Warn them about the dangers of looking directly at the sun. Can the children describe the colours they can see? Do any of the colours merge or overlap?

Return to the classroom and involve the children in limiting the collage materials to those colours observed in the sky. Challenge them to sort the collage materials into three categories — those you can see through easily (transparent), those you can see through but not clearly (translucent) and those you cannot see through at all (opaque).

What to do

Give each child a clear polythene sheet (part of a bag) and use the masking tape to stick the four corners of the sheet to the table to prevent it slipping. Invite them to use the collage materials on the polythene to create a picture of the sky based on their observations. Encourage them to consider carefully which materials to use, bearing in mind how transparent the material is as well as the colour. They will probably find it easier to put the glue on to the polythene sheet, cut or tear the material and then press it in place on the glue. Suggest they try overlapping some colours and leaving some areas empty with just the clear polythene showing.

Remove the masking tape and leave the pictures to dry. Stick a dark blue card frame around the polythene sheet using the masking tape. Although the children may be able to help measure the strips of card, an adult will need to make most of the frame. Mount some of the pictures against a window so that the light shines through and leave some for the children to experiment with. They may wish to try holding them in different places in the classroom and compare the results. They may like to try shining torches on the back of them or placing them against different coloured sugar paper to observe the effects.

Discussion

Suggest the children look through the clear polythene before it is stuck down. Remind them never to put plastic bags over their heads. While they are working, discuss the range of colours with them. Which is the darkest or lightest blue? Does the colour remind them of something else? Suggest they try to look through the various collage materials before sticking them on to their picture. How does it change what they can see? What effect does it have if they overlap two different colours? What happens to the PVA adhesive as it dries?

Evaluation

Compare and contrast the finished sky pictures. Look at those displayed against the window and ask the children which colours are transparent, translucent or opaque. Take one or two examples and ask the children to describe how the colours change when the pictures are held in different parts of the classroom, placed against coloured sugar papers and held in front of a torch. Do any of the colours become lighter or darker? Do any of the transparent colours become opaque? Which picture do they think looks most like sky and why?

Follow-up

Collect and use sunglasses and then make some with different coloured Cellophane or tissue in them. How clearly can they see through them and how do they change the colour of their environment? (Science and Technology)

Umbrellas

Objective
To explore hot and cold colours.

What you need
A collection of umbrellas (different sizes, shapes, colours/patterns, materials, purposes, for instance, golf/fishing, parasol), pale coloured sugar paper in a range of 'hot' and 'cold' colours, scissors, fabric pieces in a range of 'hot' and 'cold' colours, PVA adhesive, glue sticks, coloured chalks.

Preparation
Examine the collection of umbrellas and discuss the differences and similarities in design, the materials used, the different purposes and those suitable for winter/summer use. Focus particularly upon the overall shape, the number of sections of material when viewed from one side, any visible point at the top of the umbrella and any decoration along the edge (a border, a frill). How much of the handle can be seen and what shape is it?

Allow the children to handle the fabric pieces, identifying the colours they can see in them. Which colours make them think of a hot sunny day or a cold winter day? Can they each made a set of 'hot' and 'cold' coloured fabrics?

What to do
Ask the pupils to decide whether they are going to make a collage of a 'hot' summer umbrella or a 'cold' winter one. Suggest they bear this in mind when choosing a piece of sugar paper and a chalk. Ask them to use the chalk to map out the basic shapes of their umbrella. Stress the need to fill the paper and to avoid drawing details. Encourage them to refer back to the real umbrellas as a reminder of the shapes and proportions involved.

Invite the children to stick the fabric pieces on to their umbrella shape. They will probably find it easier to put the adhesive on to the paper and then press the fabric on top. Encourage them to make the pieces of fabric touch or overlap so there are no large empty spaces. Remind them to choose fabrics which reflect their 'hot' or 'cold' theme. Sort the children's finished umbrellas into 'hot' and 'cold' and display them along with the real models that inspired them.

Discussion
Talk with the children about the colour of the fabrics they choose. Ask them to give reasons to justify their choice. Why do they associate red with 'hot' colours?

Evaluation

Compare and discuss the final display. Ask them to identify the 'hot' summer umbrellas and the 'cold' winter ones. Which umbrella do they think is the 'hottest' or 'coldest' and why? Look at several 'hot' summer umbrellas and compare the colours and fabrics chosen. Are the same colours used in each one? Do any of the children disagree with the colours which have been chosen?

Follow-up

Make a collection of objects to show a set of 'hot' coloured objects and a set of 'cold' coloured objects. (Mathematics)

Clowns

Objective

To explore the idea of using colours to show emotions such as 'happy' and 'sad'.

What you need

Pictures of clowns, sugar paper in a range of pastel colours – pale yellow, pink or orange (for happy) and grey, pale blue or green (for sad), charcoal, coloured chalks, fixative.

Preparation

Discuss the pictures of clowns, focusing especially on their faces. Which ones look happy or sad? What colours have been used? Do these help to make the clown's face look happy or sad?

What to do

Ask the children to decide whether they are going to draw a happy or sad clown and to bear this in mind when choosing their coloured sugar paper. Invite them each to choose the chalks and charcoal which they feel will best convey the emotion of their clown. Suggest they design a large clown's head on their paper using the chalks and charcoal. More mature children can be encouraged to overlap and blend colours with their finger to create new ones. Spray the finished drawings with fixative according to the manufacturer's instructions.

Discussion

Refer the children back to the pictures of clowns for ideas for faces and hats. What shapes can they use to show their clown is sad? Which colours will make their clown look happy? Remind them to be careful not to smudge accidentally the charcoal and chalks. Can any of them describe what happens when they overlap two different coloured chalks?

Evaluation

Focus on one or two clown portraits and discuss the colours used. Have these been successful in making the clown appear happy or sad? Compare several pictures of sad clowns to see if the children have chosen similar colours. Is blue always a 'sad' colour? Do any of the children disagree with a colour which has been chosen to represent 'happy'?

Follow-up

Invite the children to write a story about their clown. What is his or her name and what happened to make him or her happy or sad? (English)

Ponds and water

Objective

To use 'The Water Lily Pond' by Claude Monet (or any other Monet painting of water lilies) as inspiration for a colour-mixing activity.

What you need

'The Water Lily Pond' by Claude Monet (copies can often be found on greetings cards, calendars, postcards and in books such as *Monet in the '90s* by Paul Hayes Tucker, Guild Publishing), white cartridge paper, brushes, palettes, water pots, a limited range of paint colours — blue, yellow, red, green, purple, white.

Preparation

If possible, take the children to look at a local pond. Discuss the colours they can see in the water, the reflections of surrounding vegetation or buildings and the surface lines created by the movement of the water. If a pond is not available, try looking at large puddles or a water tray.

Discuss 'The Water Lily Pond' by Claude Monet. What colours has the artist used? Focus on the shape and position of the bridge and the fact that it goes from one side of the picture to the other. What kind of brush strokes have been used to depict the water and which direction do they go in?

Invite the pupils to limit the range of colours to be used by referring to those in Monet's painting. Explain that Monet often preferred not to use black because it made the overall effect of the painting rather sombre. Which other colour could they use when mixing to make colours darker?

What to do

Explain to the children that they are going to try to paint a similar picture, using the same composition but mixing their own colours. Show them how to make a wash by adding water to a colour they have mixed and ask them to cover the whole of their paper with their wash. Invite them to mix another colour and paint a bridge, referring them back to Monet's painting to remind them of its shape and position. Ask them to paint the pond water, mixing a variety of different colours and using brushstrokes which imitate the directions used by Monet. When dry, display the finished paintings alongside the original Monet painting.

Discussion

Invite the pupils to describe the wash. How has the consistency or colour of the paint changed by adding water? Encourage them to look carefully at what happens to the paint used for the bridge when placed on top of wet paper. As they mix colours, ask them to describe the colours they have mixed. Are they light or dark? Which colours did they mix to achieve them? Which colours made other colours darker? Was there a colour apart from white which made colours lighter?

Evaluation

Compare the children's painting to the original Monet painting. Are there any bridges which are almost the same shape as Monet's? How are the others different? Look at one or two pictures in detail. Which colours have been used for the water? Are any of the colours the same as in the original painting? Help the children to realise that not using black has produced a much brighter painting. What kind of brushstrokes have been used for the water? What impression does this give of the water — still and calm, ruffled by a breeze or very rough?

Follow-up

Compare the styles and techniques used by other artists when painting water. Try to choose two or three very distinctive examples. What are the similarities and differences? Discuss the range of colours used and the impression this creates. Choose one or two colours in the paintings and ask the pupils which colours they think the artists mixed to achieve them. Test out their suggestions. (Art)

Fear of fire

Objective

To use 'The Scream' by Edvard Munch (or a portrait by any other artist which strongly conveys a sense of fear) to inspire drawings which use 'hot' colours to represent the emotion of fear.

What you need

A reproduction of 'The Scream' by Edvard Munch (*Edvard Munch* by U. Bischoff, Taschen Publishers — bear in mind any highly sensitive children who may find this painting disturbing), white cartridge paper, coloured pencils.

Preparation

Pupils need a great deal of discussion about fire safety and the destructive effects of fire before embarking on this activity. Show them videos and posters and read stories and poems about fire. If possible, ask a fire fighter or a Fire Prevention Officer to visit the school to talk to the children. Discuss how they would feel if they were trapped in a fire and what they would do to attract help. Many will suggest screaming as a strategy for gaining attention. Ask them to work with a partner, each one taking turns to scream while the other watches what happens to their facial features. (If the screaming becomes too noisy, ask them to mime!) How do their eyes and mouth change? Where do lines and creases appear on their faces? Does the colour of their face alter?

Show them 'The Scream' by Edvard Munch and ask them to describe how the person in the painting is feeling. Can they suggest reasons for the emotion? How has the artist painted the face to create the impression of a scream? What are the dominant colours in the painting and why should Edvard Munch choose these? Would they be suitable for drawing the face of someone trapped in a fire?

Invite the pupils to sort the coloured pencils to make a set of 'hot' colours and discuss whether they wish to include black or not.

What to do

Suggest the children use the coloured pencils to draw and colour a large, screaming face on their piece of white paper. Encourage them to look at their partner's face, miming a scream, and to include details such as wrinkles and creases. Suggest they overlap colours to create new colours and try not to leave large white spaces on the face. Display the finished drawings alongside the copy of Edvard Munch's painting.

Discussion

As the children work, talk about the colours they are using. Which is the hottest colour? What hot things do they associate with red? Can they describe any new colours they have made by overlapping the coloured pencils? What shapes or lines in their drawings, do they think are helping to convey fear?

Evaluation

Compare and contrast the children's pictures. Do the colours they have chosen influence how hot the face appears? For example, does using mostly red make a face appear hotter than one which uses mostly yellow? Which face do they think is most afraid? Which one appears to be screaming the loudest? Which parts of the drawing help to convey these feelings most? Try covering up sections of the face, such as the mouth, to see whether the effect is still as strong.

Follow-up

Ask the children to make a collection of comic-strip illustrations (in books as well as comics). Suggest they try to find examples of faces showing emotions — angry, happy, sad, frightened. How do the illustrators convey these emotions? Do they use colours (red for anger, blue for sad) to help portray these feelings?

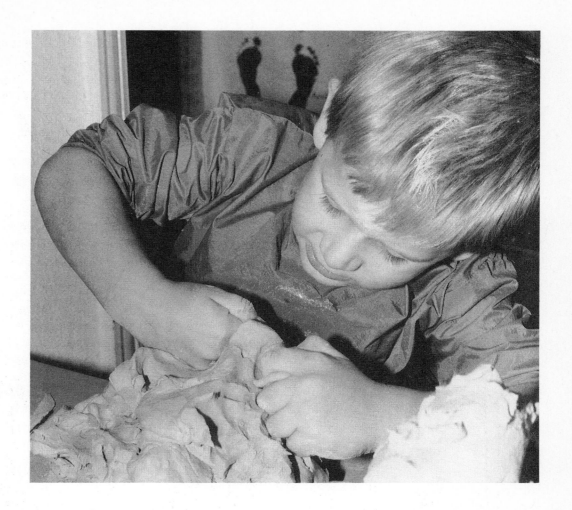

Texture

Chapter four

The sense of touch is an important means of exploring the world for a young child. Watch any group of early years pupils when meeting an unfamiliar object for the first time and their natural response is to touch, stroke and feel it. Although they intuitively explore the tactile qualities of objects, they have not necessarily acquired a vocabulary to help them describe and discriminate between textures. They will need to be deliberately introduced to words such as bumpy, rough, smooth, soft, sticky and so on.

Teaching strategies

Many common early years activities can support and extend their understanding of textures. Incidental reference may be made to how something feels when introducing a new teddy to the play house, when climbing through a plastic tunnel or when adding water to the sand tray. In fact, almost every activity can be used to focus young children's attention on the way something feels. More structured activities can help to highlight the variety of textures and help build the necessary vocabulary. Matching textures using texture dominoes or identifying objects in a 'feely' box or bag offer ideal opportunities to introduce the concept of texture.

Many artists are interested in the surface qualities of the objects in their environment and are keen to include this in their work. It may take the form of a real three-dimensional texture as found on the incised surface of a sculpture or on the raised surface of a collage. Alternatively, textures can be depicted in two dimensions when, for example, charcoal is smudged to show the fur of an animal or when paint is applied thickly to create the impression of bark on a tree.

When introducing texture to early years children, start with activities which offer them the opportunity to explore real three-dimensional textures rather than the more abstract notion of creating an illusion of texture in two dimensions. Plastic materials such as clay, play dough or Plasticine provide an excellent vehicle for investigating these surface qualities. Initially, using these materials should be seen as an experience in touching rather than a means of producing recognisable models – discovering the potential of each material is more important than the end product. Always start by

encouraging the children to use only their hands and fingers to investigate the material. Extend their vocabulary by asking what happens when they bang, squeeze, press, drop, poke, pull, twist, stretch or stroke the material. Add water to each of the materials or allow them to dry out overnight. Discuss how they have changed and compare each material's potential for modelling.

Once the children are experienced in manipulating the materials purely with their hands and fingers, tools can be introduced. These can be everyday objects and need not be expensive modelling tools. Initially, allow them to press a series of natural objects (leaves, shells, sticks, stones) or man-made objects (potato masher, fork, keys, string) into their clay. What happens if they choose one object and repeat or overlap the texture all over a piece of clay?

Collage work offers endless possibilities for exploring the tactile qualities of a whole multitude of materials such as fabrics, threads and the many forms of paper and card. Initially, tearing the collage materials may prove easier until young children have enough physical co-ordination to use scissors. Similarly, they are likely to begin by creating random arrangements of collage materials and, as they mature, gradually move to more deliberately-arranged compositions. Obviously this means appropriate tasks must be devised to suit the stage of development.

Once children have had lots of 'play' experience handling collage and plastic materials, it can be helpful to focus their attention on more specific aspects of texture. Offer them activities where they are asked to compare opposites such as rough and smooth or hard and soft. Such activities will help introduce essential vocabulary and highlight the similarities and differences between textures. It is also important for them to realise that textures can be found in both nature and the man-made environment. Children can look for texture in natural or man-made materials and use these to create texture in their own work. For example, natural materials such as seeds and leaves lend themselves to collage work while sticks and rocks could be used to create an outdoor sculpture. Similarly, man-made materials such as different papers or fabrics, yarns or string can all add texture to both two and three-dimensional work.

Texture in two and three dimensions

The above activities lead naturally into the importance of texture in three-dimensional work. When working in

three dimensions, concerned with th difficulties of cons overlook the asp such as Giants (p realise that addi interest as well dimensional eff are only introd added or appl They also need to realise that can be cut or incised into many materials. The easiest way to introduce this notion is by pressing finger nails, objects or modelling tools into plastic materials such as clay, Plasticine or play dough.

Rubbings are a useful way of introducing the more difficult concept of textures in two dimensions. Initially, allow the children to experiment by placing thin paper over a range of textured surfaces and rubbing firmly with the side of a soft wax crayon. Again, there are many suitable to choose from — both natural and man-made. Once the children have mastered the physical co-ordination skills required, they can begin to use this technique in a more structured way (as in Faces, p90).

Creating textures in two dimensions is quite a sophisticated idea so it is important to choose subject matter and media carefully. Make sure the subject has a very obvious texture such as a bumpy piece of wood or a furry teddy bear. Young children will find it much more difficult to recreate subtle textures. It is also more helpful if you can actually show them the objects and help them work from observation. Relying solely on memory is a much more difficult task. Similarly, make sure the media the children are given will easily allow them to create the texture being observed. Inappropriate media will mean that even the most skilful child will find it impossible to represent the surface quality of the object chosen.

possible look at how other
tried to show texture in their
cal potter may be able to lend
s or sculptures where texture is an
tant feature. Reproductions of
ous paintings may lend themselves to
discussion about texture. How has the
artist managed to show the roughness of
a tree trunk or the softness of clothing?

Two activities at the end of the chapter
encourage the children to make links with
other artists — Vincent Van Gogh and
Henry Moore — through a study of their
use of texture.

Christmas stockings

Objective
To distinguish between rough and smooth
surfaces.

What you need
A Christmas stocking filled with objects
with different surfaces (some rough and
some smooth), sorting hoops, brightly
coloured sugar paper in different sizes,
scissors, collage materials with various
rough and smooth textures (wallpaper,
plastic bags, coloured foil, corrugated
card, bubble wrap, crêpe paper, tissue
paper, sand paper), PVA adhesive, glue
sticks.

Preparation
Use the Christmas stocking as a 'feely
bag'. Invite children to put their hand into
the stocking, feel an object, describe it
and guess what it might be. As each
object is withdrawn, place it into a sorting
hoop using 'rough' and 'smooth' as the
criteria. The children may then bring their
own objects to put into the stocking and
so repeat the game several times. Show
the children the collage materials and
sort them into 'rough' and 'smooth' sets.

What to do

Explain to the children that they are each going to cut out a large Christmas stocking shape from sugar paper. Allow them to choose the colour and size of their paper then, once they have cut out their stocking shape, invite the children to cut or tear the collage materials and stick them on to their stocking to represent presents. Challenge them to choose the materials carefully so that some of their 'presents' feel smooth and some feel rough.

Discussion

While the children work, talk to them about the materials they are using. Which ones are easiest to tear? Which ones are hard to cut? Can they think of other words to describe the texture of the collage materials? Have they used more rough or more smooth texture?

More mature children may be able to give their stocking a more three-dimensional appearance by bending the collage materials rather than sticking them flat against the surface of the stocking while others may be capable of using scissors to give some materials a shaggy appearance.

Take the opportunity to discuss how the adhesive feels on their fingers when it is wet and compare it to glue which has dried. What other sticky substances can the children think of?

Evaluation

Discuss the finished Christmas stockings with the children. Can they point to a rough texture? How many different smooth materials can they see on one stocking? Can they think of a particular present which might have the same shape or texture? Which stocking would they like to have and why?

Follow-up

Make a flip-over book (see Figure 1) for 'as smooth as . . .' and 'as rough as . . .'. Invite the children to suggest ideas and then ask them to draw pictures to illustrate the ideas. (English)

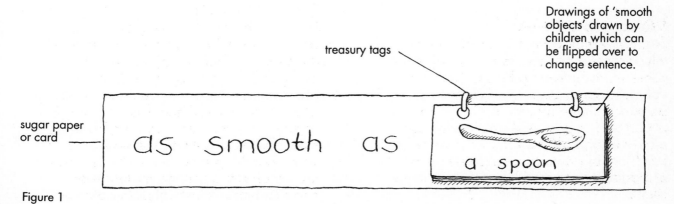

Drawings of 'smooth objects' drawn by children which can be flipped over to change sentence.

treasury tags

sugar paper or card

as smooth as

a spoon

Figure 1

The senses

Objective
To distinguish between hard and soft textures.

What you need
Thin card of various shapes and sizes, a variety of hard and soft materials such as small cardboard boxes (matchboxes, toothpaste boxes), tissue paper, cotton wool balls, small coloured fromage frais pots, coloured matchsticks, sponge, coloured sponge washing-up cloths, scissors, PVA adhesive, glue sticks.

Preparation
Suggest the children work in pairs and take turns to pretend they are blind. One child chooses a picture (a drawing or painting which they have done in the past) and challenges the other child to use their hands to feel it. What can they tell about the picture? Would the picture be very interesting to a blind person? What kind of picture would a blind person prefer?

Gather together the hard and soft materials and encourage the children to sort them into two sets. Explain that they are going to use these materials to make a picture which is interesting to feel.

What to do
Allow the children to choose the size and shape of their card. Suggest they choose one or two small boxes to stick on to the card. Invite them to choose one colour of tissue paper then tear and stick this all over the card and the boxes. Young children may find it easier to put the adhesive on to the card or boxes and then place the torn tissue on top. Ask the children to choose items from the set of soft materials and to stick them on to their 'picture'. Repeat this with the set of hard materials. Encourage the children to consider carefully where they are going to stick the collage materials.

Discussion
Can the children tell what shape the card is by feeling with their hands with their eyes shut? Are they going to stick the boxes close together or spread out? Why cover the boxes and the card with tissue paper? Would this be more important to a sighted or blind person? While the children are choosing their hard and soft materials, talk to them about their properties. Which ones change shape when you squeeze them? Which are rough or smooth? Can any of them stretch? Point out any child who is obviously organising her collage materials into a pattern, for example, making a fan shape with the matchsticks.

Evaluation

Discuss the results with the children. Which 'picture' do they think would be most interesting to a blind person and why? Can they point out the hard or soft textures on one or two of the pictures? Look at those examples where children have been more deliberate in their organisation of materials. Does this make the picture more interesting?

Follow-up

Blindfold a child and ask them to 'take their fingers for a walk' over one of the pictures. Can all the children help to invent a story to accompany the 'walking'. For example, 'My fingers are climbing up a steep step (a box) and jumping on a bouncy castle (sponge)'. (English)

Owls

Objective

To identify the textures in natural materials and use them to create texture in a collage.

What you need

A stuffed owl (or any other bird — try local museum lending services), pictures of owls, beige coloured sugar paper in two sizes, white chalk, PVA adhesive, glue sticks, scissors, a collection of natural materials such as leaves, grasses, seeds, seed pods, dried flowers, straw.

Preparation

Show the children the stuffed owl and the pictures of owls. Focus their attention on the textures. Which feathers are soft and fluffy and which are hard? Look for smooth areas on the bird (beak, eyes, claws) and compare these with the rough areas (wings, legs).

Show the children the collection of natural materials and allow them to handle them. Discuss the fact that they are all natural materials. Can they identify rough/smooth and hard/soft textures on them? Explain that they are going to use these materials to make a collage picture of an owl and encourage them to find their own natural materials to add to the collection.

What to do

Allow the children to choose the size of their sugar paper and decide which position to have it in (landscape or portrait). Display the stuffed owl and the pictures of owls near to the working area. Ask them to use the white chalk to map out lightly the main shapes of their owl. Encourage them to refer back to the

pictures and stuffed owl for ideas.
Suggest they stick the natural collage
materials on to their owl shape to create
textures. They may find it easier to put the
adhesive on to the paper and press the
natural material gently on to it. Remind
them to make the natural materials
overlap or touch so there are no empty
spaces. When they have finished
covering the owl shape, consider the
background. Do they want to continue
using the natural materials to show the
owl in a particular habitat? Display the
completed owl collages alongside the
pictures and stuffed owl.

Discussion
As they work, focus the children's
attention on the textures to be found on
the natural materials. Encourage them to
touch them gently to help identify the
surface quality. Do the materials feel the
same all over? What words would they
use to describe them? Which materials
would they select to show the soft, fluffy
feathers or the smooth, sharp claws?
Which material is the smoothest or
bumpiest?

Evaluation
Compare and contrast the finished owl
collages. Identify and describe the texture
of the materials used. Which materials
best depict the texture on the legs or the
feathers? Compare the way these
materials have been placed to create
textures on the owls. Can the children
find examples where the materials have
been overlapped or built up in layers?

Follow-up
Invite the children to make a collection of
other natural materials — shells, seaweed,
wood, rocks, pebbles, sand, soil. Suggest
they choose two or three materials and
write a detailed description of them,
including their texture. (Science)

Weaving

Objective
To identify textures in man-made
materials and use them to create textures
in a weaving.

What you need
Two or three items of clothing from the
dressing-up box made from contrasting
fabrics, a collection of different fabric
pieces, magnifying glasses, strong card
(20cm x 20cm), strips of fabric 2cm wide
and 24cm long, strong tape.

Preparation
Show the children the items of clothing
and allow them to handle them.
Encourage them to stroke, stretch and
pull the clothing. Can they find similarities
and differences in the texture of the
fabrics? Which ones are rough/smooth,
hard/soft? Are they the same on both
sides? Discuss the fact that our clothing is
made from many different materials and
then show them the collection of fabric
pieces. Once again, encourage the
children to handle and describe the
fabrics, focusing particularly on the
texture.

Discuss the fact that fabrics are man-made in that people and machines have made them. Ask the children to use magnifying glasses to find out how the fabrics are constructed and fray some fabrics at the edges to reinforce this. Explain that fabrics are made by weaving threads together — the threads running the length of the fabric are called the warp and those running across are called the weft. Use some of the strips of fabric to demonstrate the under and over structure of weaving. Explain that the children are going to make their own weaving using similar strips of fabric.

What to do

Give each child a piece of card and ask them to choose five strips of fabric to form the warp of their weaving. An adult will need to help stick these on to the card with the tape (see Figure 1). Invite the children to weave other fabric strips under and over the warp strips using their fingers. Remind them to work from top to bottom and left to right and to alternate each strip at the beginning of each row — the first weft strip goes under the first warp strip but the second weft strip must go over it. Encourage the children to choose their fabric strips according to texture so that their weaving has as many different textures as possible. When the

weaving is finished, the ends of the weft strips can be left loose and stuck on to the back of the card with tape or trimmed.

Discussion

As the children weave, talk with them about their choice of fabric strips. Can they describe how they feel? Do they prefer rough or smooth fabrics. Which is the softest fabric on their weaving? Encourage them to feel their weaving as they work. Can they tell where one fabric meets another? Do they realise they are creating a texture through the weaving process itself?

Evaluation

Look carefully at the finished weavings and discuss the textures chosen. Does one weaving use more soft fabrics than another? Has anyone tried to create a sequence by repeating one smooth fabric after one rough fabric? Which weaving would the children most like to touch and why?

Follow-up

Visit an exhibition of costumes, either contemporary or historical and look carefully at the textures of the fabrics which have been used. (Art and History)

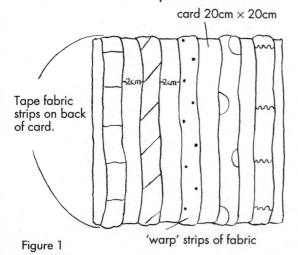

card 20cm × 20cm

Tape fabric strips on back of card.

Figure 1

'warp' strips of fabric

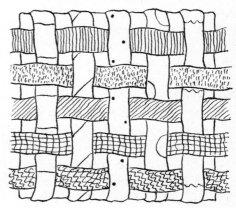

Weave the weft strips alternately under and over the warp strips.

Giants

Objective
To introduce the idea that textures can enhance a three-dimensional shape.

What you need
A collection of masks (modern card or plastic ones, examples from historical or multicultural sources such as African, American Indian or Maori), pictures of masks, strong card in bright colours, a stapler, scissors, PVA adhesive, glue sticks, materials in a wide range of textures — shredded paper, foil, corrugated card, bubble wrap, wallpaper, crêpe, tissue paper, fabrics, yarns, fur fabric, cotton wool, feathers.

Preparation
Show the children the real masks and the pictures of masks. Discuss the materials they are made from and identify any where several different materials have been used. Find any textures on the masks and talk about their purpose. Are they to give the impression of hair, wrinkled skin or a beard? Would the mask be as interesting to look at without these textures? Do they help to make the mask appear more three-dimensional?

Show the children the collection of materials and allow them to handle them. Ask them to sort them into sets according to texture — hard, soft, rough or smooth. Explain that the children are going to use these materials to make the mask of an imaginary giant.

What to do
Allow the children to choose the colour of their card and cut a strip of card to make a headband. Put the strip around each child's head and staple it together at the correct size then cut out the basic shape of the giant's face from the remaining card. Measure this against each child's face and help to cut out eye holes in the appropriate place. Invite the children to use the materials to stick features to the face such as eyes, eyebrows, nose, ears, mouth, moustache, beard, wrinkles and hair. Remind them to choose the materials according to their texture. When the masks are dry, staple them to the headband.

Discussion
As the children work, talk to them about the textures they are choosing. Which materials would be most suitable for the texture of a beard or eyebrows? Can they create suitable textures by changing the materials in some way? For example, they may decide to cut, fold or bend strips of card or paper. Will their giant have short, spiky hair or long, curly hair? Which material would best achieve this? Have they remembered to include a variety of different textures on their mask? Refer them back to the pictures and real masks for ideas.

Evaluation

Ask the children to model their masks in small groups while the rest of the class discuss them. Look for the giants which have similar features, such as a moustache, and compare the materials chosen. Are some more effective than others? Ask the children to describe the differences in texture that each material creates — card might produce a stiff, smooth moustache while shredded paper might create a soft, shaggy one. Would the masks have appeared so three-dimensional if the features had been drawn with paint or felt-tipped pens?

Follow-up

Ask the children to work in small groups to invent a short play about their giants. When they are happy with their play, ask them to wear their masks to act out a final version to the rest of the class. (Drama)

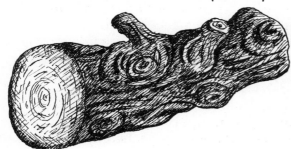

Wood

Objective

To introduce the idea that textures can be incised (cut into a surface) or applied (added on top of a surface) on to clay.

What you need

A collection of different pieces of wood, clay, wooden boards to work on, rolling pins, wooden or plastic modelling tools, a knife, a collection of objects (natural — sticks, stones, fir cones, shells; man-made — pegs, spoons, paper-clips, lids, combs).

Preparation

Introduce the idea of incised textures by making a texture matching game. Roll out a piece of clay then cut out a simple picture (such as an owl) and use several different objects to press a texture into the clay. When dry, show the clay picture to the children together with the objects and see if they can match each object to its corresponding texture.

Introduce the idea of applied textures by demonstrating how coils and small lumps of clay can be added to a flat clay surface. If the children have never used clay before, allow them a period of 'play' with the new material, encouraging them to use the rolling pins and the various objects.

Show the children the collection of pieces of wood and discuss the various textures which they can see on them. Which pieces have holes cut into them? Are there any pieces with raised bumps or ridges? Explain to the children that they are going to try to make their piece of clay look like a piece of wood.

What to do

Give each child a wooden board and a piece of clay. Ask them to use the rolling pins to roll their piece of clay flat. Suggest they use one of the modelling tools to scratch the shape of their piece of wood very faintly on to the clay. Once they are satisfied with the shape, it can be cut out with a knife. Some children may need help with this.

Encourage the children to roll out small coils of clay and press them on to their clay shape to create ridges. If the clay is very dry, slip (a mixture of clay and water) may be needed to act as a glue to stick the coil on to the clay. When the children are happy with their ridges, suggest they use the modelling tools and the various objects to press into the clay. Encourage them to choose appropriate tools and objects to create wood-like marks. Allow the clay to dry and then fire it in a kiln (either fired once to gloss temperatures or biscuit fired, glazed and then fired again). If using a glaze, choose one which will allow the textures to show through or rub on a safe oxide (iron) instead. Display the real pieces of wood with the children's work.

Discussion
Refer the children back to the real pieces of wood for ideas on the overall shape of their model. Encourage them to notice the asymmetrical shapes and to incorporate this into their own work. Talk with them when they are making the coils. Do they want short or long ones, fat or thin ones? When they press them on to their clay shape, are they going to make straight or curved ridges? Discuss the textures and marks made by each modelling tool or object. Refer them back to the real pieces of wood again for ideas on how to group the marks. Are the holes going to be grouped together or spread randomly over the clay? Are the ridges going to have any texture on them?

Evaluation
Compare and contrast the children's work. Which piece of 'clay' wood do they think is most realistic? Why? Discuss how the clay has been changed by heat in the firing. How has the colour and texture been altered? Can they identify which areas have been raised on the 'clay' wood? Which areas have been cut into by pressing in tools or objects? Can they match tools to marks?

Follow-up
Plan a similar activity with a different material such as play dough or Plasticine. Compare and contrast the activities and the response of the materials. Is it easier to make textures with clay or Plasticine? Which is the softer material? Do they change in the same ways as they dry out? (Art and Science)

Faces

Objective
To make the link between textures in three dimensions and those in two dimensions using the technique of 'rubbings'.

What you need
Large and small pieces of white cartridge paper, soft wax crayons, a collection of materials suitable for taking 'rubbings' — corrugated card, net curtains, Duplo or Lego baseboards, wallpaper with a raised surface, materials with a raised surface such as plastic netting or packaging materials, mirrors.

Preparation
Show the children the collection of materials. Encourage them to touch them and then discuss their tactile characteristics. If the 'rubbings' technique

is new to them, allow a period of experimentation with the materials before starting the assigment.

Give each child a small mirror and encourage them to study their own faces. Talk with them about the various parts of their face and the relative position of each feature.

What to do

Allow the children to choose a piece of white paper and suggest they use the wax crayons to draw the basic shapes of a face, including all the features mentioned in their discussion. Remind them to fill the paper with their drawing. Explain that they are going to colour the face using different textured materials by placing them under the picture and pressing hard with the side of a wax crayon. Firstly, ask them to choose a texture and use it to colour the background around the face. Then suggest they change textures and colour the skin on the face. Continue this activity to add other details such as hair, mouth, eyes and so on. Allow them to choose their colours either symbolically or realistically. Display the finished pictures with the materials used for taking rubbings.

Discussion

Talk about why it is better to use the crayon on its side and why it is necessary to press hard. Can they predict what sort of texture each material will make? Are they surprised by any of the results? Which colours seem to show up better? Have they forgotten to include an important feature such as hair or a mouth? Emphasise the importance of keeping the paper still as they rub. What happens if the paper moves?

Evaluation

Compare and contrast the finished pictures. Can the children match the materials to the texture created by the rubbings? Which rubbing shows up most clearly and why? Is it due to the colour chosen or the texture used? Encourage the children to feel their pictures so that they realise they only look bumpy and that the surface of the paper has not been drastically changed.

Follow-up

Invite the children to make further rubbings on several sheets of paper and then cut them up and use them for collage work, choosing their own subject matter. (Art)

Cats

Objective
To introduce the idea that media can be manipulated to give the illusion of texture.

What you need
Different sized pieces of grey sugar paper, chalks or pastels, charcoal, one or two real cats and a collection of pictures of cats, photographs of the children's pet cats.

Preparation
The quality of the children's work will be greatly enriched if they have the opportunity to meet and touch a real cat rather than rely solely on pictures. (Be aware of animal allergies and the problems these may cause.) Name the various body parts of the cats and discuss how these relate to each other. Compare and contrast their different colours and especially the texture of their fur.

Use the pastels or chalks to experiment on small pieces of sugar paper. What marks would they use to make something look fluffy or smooth? Can they suggest alternative media?

What to do
Explain to the children that they are going to draw a large cat, either one which has visited the class or one which they know well. Allow them to choose the size of their sugar paper and whether they want it to be in the landscape or portrait position. They must use their pastels or chalks to show the cat's texture. Is it long-haired and fluffy all over? Is it mostly smooth coated or does it have some areas which are shaggy?
Stress the importance of not leaning on their picture by mistake but suggest they might like to smudge areas deliberately to increase the impression of fur.

Discussion
Remind them of the real cats or refer them back to the pictures if they have trouble remembering all the body parts. Encourage them to draw their cat as large as possible so that it fills most of the picture space. Talk about the colours they are using and suggest they overlap the pastels to create new colours. How are they making their cats appear smooth or fluffy? Are they using straight or curved lines or smudging?

Evaluation
Discuss the finished pictures with the children. Which cats are lying down or standing up? How many black cats are there? Choose two or three different cats and discuss their various textures. How have they been made to look smooth or fluffy? Which cat would the children like to stroke and why?

Follow-up
Read the poem 'This is the hand' by Michael Rosen (*A First Poetry Book* J. Foster, OUP) and use it to inspire a class poem about cats. Ask the children for suggestions and then invite them to illustrate their ideas for a zigzag book. For example, This is the hand that . . . stroked a fluffy cat, tickled a black cat's tummy, threw a ball for a cat to chase, put the cat food into the bowl and so on. (English)

Flowers

Objective
To use 'The Sunflowers' (or any other flower painting) by Vincent Van Gogh to inspire a painting incorporating texture.

What you need
A large print of 'The Sunflowers' by Vincent Van Gogh (look for examples on greetings cards, postcards, calendars and books such as *Van Gogh* by W. Uhde, Phaidon), white cartridge paper, real sunflowers (if possible), different sized brushes, water pots, a limited range of paints to match the print (for example, red, yellow, green, brown, white), palettes, sand, sawdust or wood shavings, PVA adhesive.

Preparation

Discuss the painting and encourage the children to name the range of colours used. Take the opportunity to involve the children in limiting their paints to only those colours used by Van Gogh. Choose one or two colours in the painting and ask the children to suggest which colours could have been mixed together to make them. Explain that Van Gogh often applied his oil paints in thick layers to build up a rough texture on his paintings. Can the children identify areas in the picture which they think would have been thick and bumpy on the original painting? If real sunflowers are available, show these to the children and compare them with Van Gogh's painting. Are they the same colour, size, shape and texture?

What to do

Explain to the children that they are going to paint their own version of Van Gogh's painting. Give them a piece of white paper and ask them to mix a colour for the background. Show them how to add water to make a wash and paint this all over their white paper. Then ask them to mix another colour to paint the vase and continue mixing colours to paint the flowers. Draw their attention to the table in 'The Sunflowers' picture and ask them to paint their vase on top of a table.

Allow the paintings to dry and suggest the children return to their paintings to add a thick textured paint to only a few selected places in their pictures. Encourage them to mix a colour and then stir in PVA adhesive together with either sand or wood shavings. Once they have used their own textured paint, they can swap with someone else. Display the finished paintings with the original painting that inspired them.

Discussion

While they are painting, discuss which sized brush is appropriate. Is a thin brush suitable for painting on the wash? Also, refer them back for details to the original painting and the real flowers if available. Talk with them about the colours they are mixing. Can they find the colour they have just mixed in Van Gogh's painting?

When mixing the textured paint, encourage them to talk about how the sand or sawdust changes the paint. Why is the PVA adhesive needed? When applying the textured paint, prompt them to consider which sized brush will be most suitable. Very young children will be tempted to paint the thick texture randomly, possibly obliterating most of the previous painting. Sensitively, try to encourage them to be more selective and apply the texture in two or three areas only. When they swap paints, ask them to describe the similarities and differences in the paint.

Evaluation

Discuss the children's pictures, paying particular attention to the colours they have used. Can they match any of their own colours to those in the original painting? Focus on the textured areas in their paintings. Can they tell which paint has sand or wood shavings in it? Do the textured areas have any other differences? For example, the PVA adhesive makes some paints shiny.

Follow-up

Allow the children to experiment mixing their own textured paints using materials which they have suggested, such as soil, lentils, grass. Which ones work well or badly? Can they explain why? Encourage them to use their own textured paints to create a painting of their own choice. (Art)

Guinea pigs

Objective

To look at the techniques used by Henry Moore to create texture and link them with the children's drawings of guinea pigs.

What you need

A copy of one of Henry Moore's Sheep Sketches (from *Henry Moore's Sheep Sketchbook*, Thames & Hudson), a real guinea pig (or any other pet), pictures of guinea pigs, white cartridge paper, black pens.

Preparation

Show the children the real guinea pig and allow them to touch and hold it. (Be aware of animal allergies and the problems these may cause.) Talk about the various body parts and how they relate to each other. Discuss its overall shape, colour and texture. Link the discussion about the real guinea pig to any pictures. Is the real one exactly the same as the one in the picture? How is it different?

Talk about the drawing of a sheep by Henry Moore. What medium has the artist used? Look in detail at the marks he has used to draw the sheep and bring their attention to the way he has created the impression of the texture of their fleece. If pens are an unfamiliar medium, give the children some scrap paper and suggest they experiment with drawing similar marks.

What to do
Ask the children to use the black pens to draw a large picture of a guinea pig on their piece of white paper. Refer them to the real guinea pig and encourage them to include details from their observations. Also display the drawings by Henry Moore nearby and use them when talking with the children.

Discussion
As they draw, talk about the various body parts of the guinea pig. Have they drawn the correct number of legs? What shape are the guinea pig's eyes? Discuss how they are going to show the texture of the fur. Will they use long curved lines, short spiky marks or try cross-hatching?

How can they show different coloured markings on the guinea pig's fur? Invite the children to look again at Henry Moore's drawings to see how he solved similar problems. Can they use similar marks to create the fur on their guinea pigs?

Evaluation
Look carefully at the children's drawings and talk about the different marks made to represent fur. Can they find four different methods amongst their pictures? Which marks are most successful in creating the texture of fur? Compare the marks made by the children to those used by Henry Moore. What are the similarities and differences?

Follow-up
Look at the illustrations in story books and find examples of furry animals. What media have the artists used and how have they tried to represent the texture of fur? Illustrators such as Brian Wildsmith, Charles Keeping, Suzanna Gretz and Jill Murphy all use different techniques and media. Compare and contrast examples by two of them. (Art)